Sylvia M Everitt's
Staffordshire Millennium Embroideries

History by
Dianne Mannering

CHURNET VALLEY BOOKS
43 Bath Street, Leek, Staffordshire. 01538 399033
email: picture.book@virgin.net web: freespace.virgin.net/c.hinton/
© Dianne Mannering, Sylvia Everitt and Churnet Valley Books 1999
ISBN 1 897949 62 6

Printed in Malta by Interprint Limited

To Sylvia

Acknowledgements

Many thanks to my husband Richard who spent hours editing the manuscript. Also Val Turner (née Hale when we were at Cronehills School together), who trawled through the manuscript before Richard had it, altering all the things that make him cross, like fare/fair, tail/tale, fate/fete. And to my daughter, Polly who 'went metric' for me.

Many other people have been willing and cheerful in their help.
I would like to especially thank:

Stan Hill - The Blackcountry Society and editor of The Blackcountryman who provided much information on the 19th century. John Brimble - Tipton Community Heritage Project, particularly for the Zeppelin raids.
Sue Whitehouse - Regeneration and Environment Group, Wolverhampton Metropolitan Borough Council. The Cotswold Farm Park. Express & Star. John Giffard of Chillington Hall. Lichfield Tourist Information Office where someone waded through files of old newspaper cuttings for me. Dudley Zoo. Major Ted Green at the Staffordshire Regimental Museum. Bass Museum. Marni Shapiero, Wedgwood. Lending libraries, reference libraries and archive departments at Lichfield, Stafford, Wolverhampton and particularly West Bromwich, where Lisa sorted out my Victoria Crosses for me and stayed late to fax through the information. Stoke City Football Club. Hednesford FC. Walsall FC. Wolverhampton Wanderers FC. Reliant Cars Ltd. South Staffordshire Water PLC.
Cath Walton, Jim Pennington and Roger Small.

Photographs of the Embroideries by Graham Beckley LBIPP

FOREWORD

I was most impressed when I saw Sylvia Everitt's Staffordshire Millennium Embroideries at the exhibition in Dudley Town Hall in September.

There is such an incredible quality of research and craftmanship here, it seems to me that these embroideries need wide publicity. It would be a shame if they were confined to Sylvia's native Staffordshire because they have a nationwide appeal.

I was asked if they would be tomorrow's antique. Oh yes, I feel sure; most certainly.

Yours sincerely

Henry Sandon

Photograph by Les Millington.

Introduction

The idea for the embroideries came to me during the Spring of 1994 when I was watching a television programme asking people to think of ideas to celebrate the Millennium. People were suggesting all the usual things like fountains and statues, which all sounded rather corporate to me, with little scope for the individual voice. I thought, "how about a tapestry - a sort of Bayeux tapestry incorporating a thousand years of Staffordshire's history?" Then I remembered that the Bayeux was in excess of 230 feet long! "Well, perhaps a mini-Bayeux tapestry", I thought.

In that second I was committed, and the Staffordshire Millennium Embroideries were conceived. I quickly knew that I wanted to encapsulate one thousand years of history on ten separate panels, each representing a century, and that I would also have a panel showing a map of Staffordshire in Tudor times, with the main towns and roads. I knew I would use twelve point canvas as a base, that there would be borders à la Bayeux - I like the Bayeux Tapestry, and that, as a tribute to English medieval needlecraft, I would edge the panels with opus Anglicorum strap work. For the vignettes I would adopt the technique much loved of the Elizabethan and Jacobean embroiderers, appliqué slipwork, which is worked on a much finer canvas than the base. These vignettes would nestle into their background of deep colour giving the panel the effect of a stained glass window in a church.

I was already to go - or so I thought. I hadn't reckoned with the enormous amount of research that would be involved. Born and bred in Hednesford, now part of Cannock, I thought I knew my Staffordshire history well. So I did - up to a point - but a point miserably short of what I needed to design my embroideries. I would estimate a quarter of all the time taken to produce the panels has been taken up with historical research. In fact, because of all the historical content of the embroideries people have often assumed that I must have been a schoolteacher - well, no, I was a wages clerk.

You will have noticed that I refer to my work as embroideries, not tapestries. Originally tapestries - the sort that hang on the walls of stately homes - were woven on looms. Today's 'tapestries' are more correctly termed canvas work, or needlepoint using a variety of canvas work stitches. But the Millennium panels are far more intricately worked than this, a variety of stitches, techniques and materials being employed, and with between ten and fifteen individual cameos separately embroidered before being appliquéd to the main canvas. I would like the work to be known as the Staffordshire Millennium Embroideries but I feel I am swimming against the tide, because the media, who are now taking a great interest in my work, seem to think anything long and embroidered is a tapestry - and their voice is louder than mine!

From the very start I intended these embroideries to be my gift to the County. However, I had not been working on them very long before I realised that it was going to be an extremely expensive undertaking and I decided that I would have to seek some sponsorship. I am very grateful to those companies and organisations who put their faith in me and 'put their hand in their pocket' to sponsor a panel. I have given each of them a thank you in the form of a representation of their logo or some other mention on the panel. My own bank in Hednesford, the HSBC (Midland Bank), sponsored the twelfth century panel and their logo is included at the top. It is amazing how many people have questioned whether the Midland Bank has been established that long!

I was probably naive. I had assumed that the embroideries would be given a home in the County town when their Millenium tour finishes - although goodness knows when that will be as it is already booked well into 2001! However Stafford County Council were unable to accommodate my gift and Lichfield stepped into the void offering a permanent home in the lovely St Mary's Centre, right in the Market Square with Dr Johnson to guard over them. When St Mary's church became 'redundant' 20 years ago, and was in danger of being developed into a supermarket or a similar, unsympathetic commercial enterprise, a group of concerned people formed a registered charity, with the intention of preserving the building - and using it, as far as possible within a Christian concept, for the benefit of the community and visitors to the City. The scheme, which eventually materialised as St Mary's Centre, leaves one third of the building as St Mary's church, and provides, on the ground floor, a social centre for senior citizens, a coffee shop and a gift shop. A mezzanine floor built within the body of the church provides a home for the Lichfield Heritage Exhibition and Treasury and is an integral part of the Centre. It is here, in a purpose built area, that the embroideries will eventually come to rest when they have finished their travels.

One question I am frequently asked is "where did you learn to embroider?" The simple answer is that I am completely self-taught. My hobby through the years has been painting, and I discovered embroidery only 15 years ago. I found that I have a natural affinity with the needle and can make it do whatever I want - perhaps something to do with the fact that when I went to school they found I was naturally left-handed and could mirror write. Even though I was made to write from left to right across the page and to use my right hand, I have the ability to use both hands with equal dexterity and can work on the canvas from any angle with equal ease.

It never occurred to me that the embroideries would attract the attention they have - and certainly, never, in my wildest dreams, did I imagine that they would spawn a book. By the time Dianne Mannering first saw the panels at the Black Country Society's local history fair in Dudley, the idea of a book had been put to me by several people. But Dianne didn't just mention it. She telephoned, she chivvied, she bullied, she nagged - "Go on, Sylvia, let me write your book." Eventually, worn down and amused by her eagerness, I agreed, although I wasn't at all sure that any publisher would want to print a book that pivoted on my embroideries. I am particularly pleased that Dianne is herself a Staffordshire woman - "a born and bred Black Country wench" as she puts it - so both the embroideries and the book come from the heart.

Sylvia Mary Everitt

10th September 1999

The County Map

The County Map

Sylvia designed the County Map panel to sit between the 15th and 16th centuries, and the roads marked are those in use upto Tudor times. She uses some of the motifs on this panel as personal acknowledgements.

Roads, Rivers, Towns and Roman Forts

The contours of Staffordshire changed very little in the thousand years preceding the Local Government Reorganisation Act of 1972 (put into effect 1974). As all but the final twenty eight years of this millennium history relate to the period prior to these changes, I think we can safely ignore them without causing confusion.

The old Roman roads are marked in gold thread. Watling Street, now mainly the A5 trunk road, crosses the county from east to west. Ryknild Street, which is now paralleled by the A38, crosses Watling Street at Wall, a small village not far from Lichfield. The road depicted in the north of the map - which was also known as Ryknild Street, ran across the county from Rocester to the Roman fortress at Chesterton, but once the fortress lost its importance so too did the road.

Although we have given the Romans credit for these roads, there would have been well worn paths meandering across the region a thousand years or so before these invaders arrived to impose their straight roadmaking techniques upon us.

Bronze thread indicates sixteenth century tracks and many of these have survived today as our main trunk roads - for example the Stafford Road, now the A449, from Wolverhampton to Stafford.

The ribbons of blue thread represent the rivers and you will see that we appear to have two River Tames. This is because the Tame disappears over the border of the County around the area of the Tamworth jewel and wanders back into Staffordshire again near the Walsall jewel.

The pearls set into a diamond shape represent the Roman forts, stations and settlements which were established and thriving around a thousand years before Sylvia's panels begin to tell their history.

Sylvia found it impractical to try and embroider inordinately long names such as Newcastle-Under-Lyme, Wolverhampton, West Bromwich and Burton-on-Trent onto the map, and instead she has used jewels to pick out her towns and villages. The map following, taken from the panel, is a key to the places so marked.

Roads, Rivers, Roman Forts

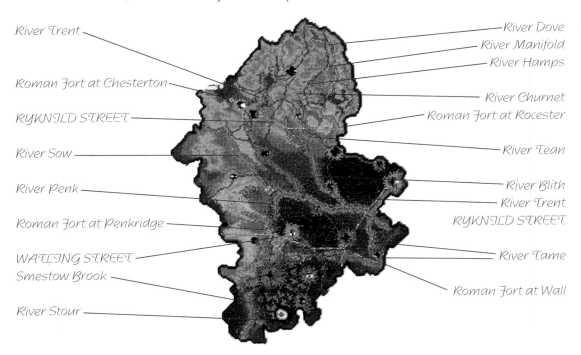

River Trent

Roman Fort at Chesterton

RYKNILD STREET

River Sow

River Penk

Roman Fort at Penkridge

WATLING STREET

Smestow Brook

River Stour

River Dove

River Manifold

River Hamps

River Churnet

Roman Fort at Rocester

River Tean

River Blith

River Trent

RYKNILD STREET

River Tame

Roman Fort at Wall

Towns and Villages

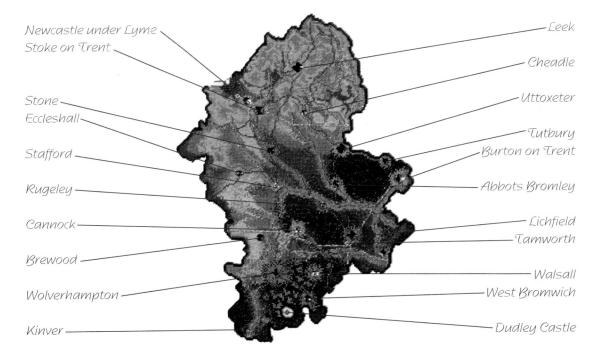

Newcastle under Lyme
Stoke on Trent

Stone

Eccleshall

Stafford

Rugeley

Cannock

Brewood

Wolverhampton

Kinver

Leek

Cheadle

Uttoxeter

Tutbury

Burton on Trent

Abbots Bromley

Lichfield

Tamworth

Walsall

West Bromwich

Dudley Castle

By the middle of the nineteenth century Staffordshire had become a huge industrial county with all the attendant problems of surging population growth and an insufficiently regulated social structure. Between 1801 and 1901 the population increased by almost a million from just over 242,000 to 1,234,500 people, making it the fourth largest county in England.

The 1888 Local Government Act gave Staffordshire the authority to form a new County Council, and Sylvia chose to depict the Staffordshire County Council coat of arms with its motto 'THE KNOT UNITES' in acknowledgement of this great stride forward towards a modern, structured and civilised society.

Staffordshire's 56 mile (90km) length and 38 mile (61km) breadth can be roughly divided into three terrains, the hilly north, the picturesquely verdant middle, and the flat south, where deposits of coal and iron fostered the industrial revolution.

The two allegorical figures, the shepherd and the coal miner, represent the mainstay of the County's livelihood during the past thousand years - agriculture and industry.

Note the small cream circle tipped with a green dot at the southern end of the map. The cream circle is the old Borough of Dudley - alien soil, that by an ancient territorial quirk belonged to Worcestershire, prior to 1965 rationalisation. However, the green dot in the centre of the cream circle denotes Dudley Castle, which from the time of the Norman Conquest belonged to Staffordshire.

William the Conqueror established his native feudal system here in England soon after 1066, whereby the land all belonged to him and he doled it out to his Norman friends and relations in return for military or fiscal services. These new landholders were the King's tenants-in-chief. They had far more land than they could cope with, so they sublet to their friends and relations, who in turn also sublet. Thus the tenant farmer owed allegiance to the Lord of the Manor who owed allegiance to the Baron in his castle, who owed allegiance to the King.

One Baron was William Ansculf of Dudley Castle. It seems that when William the Conqueror visited the middle of his new kingdom he noticed the strategic position of Dudley as a gateway to the south-east via the Tame valley, and the south-west via the Severn valley. To protect his interests he had a fortress built atop Dudley hill, it is assumed around 1069 when Staffordshire was rebelling against him. The Saxon, Earl Edwin of Mercia, who had not thrown his lot in with the anti-Norman rebels, still retained his vast lands, including Dudley in Worcestershire. Nearby Sedgley in Staffordshire was a royal estate, so William simply transferred the Castle and Castle Hill to Sedgley - and the tiny green speck in the centre of the cream circle is this piece of Staffordshire in the centre of Dudley, Worcestershire.

A few years later Earl Edwin came out on the side of the rebels and was killed. William acted quickly to forestall more trouble in the area and created the Barony of Dudley, endowed it with the late Earl Edwin's estates, and presented them, along with the castle, to his trusted henchman, William Ansculf. Ansculf's daughter married Fulke de Paganel who came into possession of the castle and many of his lands. Gervase de Paganel, Fulke's grandson, owned the castle by 1161 when he founded the Priory at Dudley. However, in 1174, Gervase backed the wrong side in a revolt against King Henry II, and the castle, a wooden construction, was dismantled as a punishment. A peace offering of 500 marks calmed Henry's ruffled feathers, and Gervase was allowed to rebuild part of the castle as an unfortified manor house. This is how it remained for the next 100 years until the Paganel line ran out and John de Somery, marrying the female Paganel heir, obtained the unsplendid remains of Dudley Castle.

John de Somery prospered and began to fortify the castle again, but with his death in 1321 the castle and estates passed to his sister's husband, John de Sutton, and remained with that family - who changed their name to Dudley - for the next 400 years. The last Dudley, Edward, was a womanising profligate who had 11 illegitimate children, but only one legitimate son to secure the line. The son died, and by 1628 Edward Dudley had became so financially embarrassed that he was forced to trade his castle, his estates and his granddaughter to a London goldsmith named Humble Ward.

The castle became a Royalist garrison during the Civil War and afterwards it was slighted and made untenable. Then, on 24th July 1750 the buildings caught fire. The conflagration lasted for three days and the lead from the roof ran red-hot down the hill setting fire to the long grass, giving the appearance that the whole hillside was alight. Thus the mighty Dudley Castle was rendered a ruin.

The cameo depicting books, ink pot and quill pen, is a tribute to some of Staffordshire's prominent men and women of the arts: Dr Samuel Johnson, the lexicographer; Izaak Walton the fisherman and writer; David Garrick the actor; Anna Seward, The Swan of Lichfield, poetess and letter writer; and Mary Ann Evans - George Eliot

Sylvia also pays tribute to historians M W Greenslade and D G Stuart, whose book 'A History of Staffordshire' was her constant companion for the five and a half years that her panels took to research and embroider. Rosemary Knight, a poetess and great friend of Sylvia's, who gave her cheerful encouragement when the panels seemed a never ending task, has her name embroidered onto a book spine, guaranteeing her a little, unexpected, immortality. As anyone who has been following the making of the Staffordshire Millennium Embroideries will know, this panel has been substantially reworked after Sylvia decided that she didn't want the map on its original blue background. The night before the newly refinished map was due to be photographed I noticed that one of the books was without a name on its spine and I mentioned to Sylvia that she wasn't quite finished even at this eleventh hour. When I saw the photograph a few days later, I realised why. I am much flattered to have my name embroidered into posterity; thank you Sylvia.

The 10 'century' panels have a set format. The borders always give the names of the Kings and Queens who ruled, although for most their interests in Staffordshire extended to little more than hunting in the forests here. The borders also contain the typical flora and fauna of Staffordshire, and in the later panels show notable people connected with the County.

The motif at the top left and the bottom right inside the main body of the panel is usually worked in silver or gold leather, and is in most cases linked to an event of great national importance. However there are no hard and fast rules, and as Sylvia crafted her panels she was not above allowing whimsy to rule.

At the end of alternate chapters Sylvia has given some brief details of the making of each panel. But if you really want to appreciate her fantastic work come along to one of the exhibitions or one of her talks.

And so to the eleventh century ....

The County Map Embroidery Details

The stitches in the background are rice, cross, tent and satin stitch blocks, worked both ways to give a textural effect. It is worked in embroidery cotton of two shades into wool of three shades, with the intention of giving the panels the effect of stained glass windows.

The Borough coat of arms was worked on 28 count canvas to allow for the amount of intricate detail required.

I am frequently asked whether the jewels of the strap work and the map were glued into place, but, in fact, they are embroiderer's stones which have small holes for attaching them.

The Eleventh Century

Kings and Queens of the Century

Ethelred II ('the Unready') reigned 978-1016. Married (1) Elfleda (2) Emma of Normandy.

Swain (Falkbeard) 1014 King of Norway.

Edmund II (Ironside) reigned 1016 for seven months. Ethelred's son by his first wife, Elfleda.

Canute (Cnut) reigned 1016-1035. Swain's son. He married (1) Elgiva of Northampton (2) Emma of Normandy - the widow of Ethelred II.

Harold (Harefoot) reigned 1035-1040. Canute & Elgiva's son.

Hardicanute reigned 1040-1042. Canute & Emma's son.

Edward (the Confessor) reigned 1042-1066. Ethelred & Emma's son. He married Edith, the daughter of Godwin, the Earl of Wessex.

Harold II reigned for nine months in 1066. Son of Earl Godwin and brother-in-law of Edward the Confessor.

William I (the Conquerer) reigned 1066-1087. Married Matilda of Flanders. William was the illegitimate son of the Duke of Normandy. He claimed that Edward the Confessor, to whom he was distantly related, had promised him the English throne, but when Edward died, the Witan (council) elected Harold as the next King.

William II (Rufus) reigned 1087-1100. Son of William I. He was killed by an arrow while hunting - he had no issue.

There were ten rulers during the century, eight prior to the Norman conquest, so perhaps William the Conqueror brought a certain orderliness with him that we may not otherwise have achieved for many centuries.

The borders

In St Peters Churchyard, Wolverhampton, stands the finest example of a Saxon churchyard cross in the whole of England.

Before churches were built, a cross would sometimes be erected to mark a site where the local people could congregate to listen to itinerant preachers who were, from the seventh century, travelling throughout Mercia converting the pagan population to Christianity.

We do not know exactly how old Wolverhampton's cross is, but we can be confident that it has been standing for at least a thousand years. It would originally have been taller than its present 4.5 metre (15 ft) because a cross head would almost certainly have sat above the cap stone, although no tell-tale fragments of any such superstructure have ever been found.

Wolves and wild boar were indigenous creatures roaming freely through the forests, which, at this time, covered ninety percent of Staffordshire. Due to persistent hunting and loss of habitat as the forests were cleared, both of these animals were believed to be extinct by the mid-thirteenth century. However, a few isolated pockets must have survived because Ralph Basset, Baron of Drayton and Lord of the Manor of Walsall, who lived until the last decade of the fourteenth century, is reputed to have slain a wild boar on Bassets Heath.

Rabbits, though, were newcomers, introduced by the Normans who prized them highly for their meat and also for their fur which was used to line cloaks and robes. In fact, the conquerors guarded their rabbits jealously, with special warrenders appointed to look after them. If your name is Warren or Warrender it is likely that your ancient forebears were rabbit keepers, and if you live in an area known as Coneygre (such as at Tipton) then you may be living on a site where the Lord of the Manor kept his rabbits.

Dudley Zoo (housed in the grounds of Dudley Castle) is actively involved in a national conservation programme, Red Alert, which is aimed at reversing the sorry plight of our red squirrels. A more serious problem than the fight for tree space which the squirrels face, is a virus passed on by their bigger, stronger North American 'tree rat' cousins.

It is thought that there may still be a very small remnant population of red squirrels on Cannock Chase, but unless some method is found of controlling the grey squirrel's breeding habits and stamping out the virus they carry, then the outlook for these pretty little creatures is bleak.

The Panel

The Opening Motif

A smiling, golden sun opens Sylvia's eleventh century panel as her personal 'hello and welcome' to everybody who has taken the time to ponder over her labour of love, crafted to tell an intriguing and enlightening tale of the history of her native Staffordshire.

The primitive face of the Green Man with foliage sprouting from his mouth represents the old Celtic nature religion. The Celts landed in England around two and a half thousand years ago and they were possibly the first humans to permanently occupy the middle of the country when they settled in Harborne, which aeons later became part of the County of Staffordshire. As the area gradually became more peopled, other religions were introduced, sometimes by stealth and sometimes by force, but the Green Man was never quite vanquished. If you take the trouble to look for him, you will recognise his floriferous face embodied in the stonework of ancient Christian churches and you can also find his effigy transposed on to plaques and other bric-a-brac in local craft shops and chintzy curtained tea-rooms. Think also of the number of pubs bearing his name - at Swindon, Kingswinford, Clifton Campville, the Leek Moorlands.......

Another hangover from the prehistoric past is the Abbots Bromley Horn Dance. Little is known for certain about the origins of this ceremony which is performed

annually in and around the village, ending at Blithfield Hall. The Abbot of Bromley granted hunting rights in Needwood Forest in the twelfth century and it is supposed that the dance, much altered to suit changing needs and fancies, may date from then. The six sets of horns are the antlers of reindeer as opposed to the indigenous roe, fallow or red deer that roamed the forests of medieval Staffordshire, and, as reindeer disappeared from Britain about eight hundred years ago, this bolsters the theory of the ceremony's twelfth century origin. It is no mean feat for the six dancers who wear the ungainly and heavy horns, the largest pair weighing 25 lb (11.4 Kg) and spanning 97cm (39 inches).

Sylvia has used an ancient type way-marker stone to show the County's five old administrative divisions, commonly known nowadays as the Ancient Hundreds. Early settlers were given a hide of land which was sufficient to support a man and his family. There was no exact science involved in the size of these hides, as a larger plot would be required to provide for the settler's needs in a bleak upland area than in the fertile valleys. For administrative purposes the hides were bundled into groups of a hundred families. These 'Hundreds' held a regular meeting called a moot where grievances were heard, criminals tried and taxes collected.

Each Hundred took its name from some physical object that could easily be identified by strangers to the area - there were no A-Zs in those days! As a 'low' was a burial place, Totmanslow and Offlow were burial grounds; in fact, Offlow may perhaps hold the site of King Offa's barrow or grave. Seisdon was possibly derived from Saxon's Hill as the word dun was Anglo-Saxon for hill. Of the five Saxon names, only Seisdon and Totmanslow remain in use.

St Chad, the patron saint of Lichfield Cathedral, was Bishop of Mercia, the Midland Kingdom, in the seventh century when he built his original church at Stowe, a little way from Lichfield. Chad's building would have been constructed of wood and stone, and Sylvia has depicted him here in the eleventh century, purely under poetic licence, to acknowledge the fact that a cathedral existed in Lichfield well before the imposing structure that is there now.

During the two and a half years that Chad was

Bishop he brought together the two warring races of the area, the conquering Angles and the subjugated Britons, thus beginning the unity of the Church of England.

Chad died in 672 and, as a shrine to him, Bishop Hedda built a church at Lichfield on the spot where the Cathedral now stands.

With the coming of Christianity came the first monasteries, but these were plundered and destroyed by the Danes who had been making a thorough nuisance of themselves around the coasts of England with their marauding pagan ways since the eighth century. They eventually breached Staffordshire in 874 and ransacked the religious houses forcing their inhabitants to flee.

As these establishments provided some basic form of care for the sick, alms for the very poor and shelter for the traveller, their wanton destruction would have caused widespread distress and a step backwards in social development.

However a monastic revival began in the area, in 1002, with the founding of a Benedictine Abbey at Burton-on-Trent. The Abbey's benefactor was an immensely wealthy Saxon, Wulfric Spot, who helped the foundation to support itself by bestowing several of his own manors including Burton, Whiston and Okeover. The monks farmed their endowment as efficiently as the methods of the day would allow and cleared trees to provide grazing for sheep. They also discovered that the special quality of Burton well water produced a most wholesome beer which prominent local families were pleased to purchase in bulk, thus providing the monks with an added income.

At the beginning of the century the Anglo-Saxon peasant-farmers lived alongside their thanes (a Saxon noble) enjoying a form of freedom which was to disappear entirely with the coming of William the Conqueror and the introduction of his Norman feudalism. Sylvia has depicted these pre-feudal days with Leofric, the Earl of Mercia at the time of Edward the Confessor, and his wife Lady Godiva (she who made the legendary ride, naked, through the streets of Coventry) at their favourite Hall House in Kings Bromley. The idea of an indoor staircase had not yet taken root and stone steps on the outside of the Hall lead up to a first floor entrance.

Leofric's grandson, Edwin, Earl of Mercia and the most powerful lord in the Midlands, played a part in King Harold's defeat at Hastings by being in the wrong place at the wrong time. Northumbria had broken out against Harold's brother, Earl Tostig, insisting that they should be governed by Edwin's brother Morcar, so Harold marched his troops up to Yorkshire to settle matters. While he was there, he took Edwin and Morcar's sister as his wife in an effort to cement better relations between himself and these two powerful earls. Tostig was obviously upset - his brother had not only sided with Edwin and Morcar against him and given away his realm, but he had even married into the opposition's family! He called upon the Kings of Scotland and Norway to help fight his corner, and so Edwin, seeing his brother's new realm under threat, marched his men up north to his aid. Tostig's supporters won the ensuing battle and King Harold was forced to march to York to protect his own northern kingdom. A few days later, on 25th September 1066, another battle took place in which both Tostig and the King of Norway were killed and Harold was the victor.

Unfortunately, this family infighting up north came at a time when Harold would have been better employed guarding his southern coasts, for Duke William of Normandy, taking advantage of Harold's absence, landed without opposition at Pevensy in Sussex on 1st October. So, having just marched his soldiers north, Harold was forced to turn tail and march them to the south.

Many of his best fighting men had been killed and he was not able to scrape together a force of infantry and militiamen until he passed through the southern shires. William's army, especially his cavalry, were better trained, and of course, not in the battle weary state of Harold's men. On 14th October, with Harold slain, Duke William became King William I of England.

The central cameo of the panel depicts William the Conqueror's harrying of Staffordshire. Robust of spirit and contentedly insular in our land-locked domain, we rebelled against the new rule in 1069 and again the following year. The second time that William was obliged to bring his troops down upon us, he made sure that there would be no need for a third visit. The villages and hamlets were torched and the inhabitants murdered. The destruction was so systematic, widespread and ruthless that the survivors died of famine as the crops and livestock had been destroyed and the farm implements and provisions collected into heaps and set alight.

To make sure that there was no more trouble William instructed a castle to be built in Stafford, but it seems that this wasn't necessary because twenty years later, when the Doomsday register was compiled, the castle - which would have been a wooden building, was a ruin and the scribe's entry for the county stated that it was poor, desolate and of no account.

The deathbed ramblings of the conquering Norman king portray a man about to meet his maker with an unsettled conscience as he tells those gathered about him: *"........much as human ambition is disposed to triumph in such successes, I am prey to cruel fears and anxieties when I reflect with what barbarities they were accompanied."*

It is to Ordericus Vitalis that we owe this insight into William's troubled state of mind, though Sylvia insists I mention that this monkish chronicler was not actually at the King's deathbed; in fact, he was writing in the twelfth century ...... and William died in 1083.

The deer represents the five forests of Staffordshire; Kinver, Brewood, Cannock, Needwood and in the north, New Forest. Two of these, Brewood and New Forest had more or less disappeared by the end of the 11th century as the population began gradually to increase and land was brought under cultivation.

A forest at this time was not just a densely wooded area, it would include open spaces, scrub and barren land too, and was, in effect, a tract of country preserved as a royal hunting ground with an important hierarchy of foresters paid to maintain it. Richard Chenvin was one such forester and he enjoyed a position of wealth and power as Keeper of Cannock Forest where his remit was to increase the forest stock and guard against poaching. Richard's situation is interesting in that he was the son of a Saxon thane and therefore one of the very few Saxons who managed to hold on to his position and property after the Conquest.

To Staffordshire folk, the words 'Cannock Forest' sound clumsy on the tongue as we are used to calling it Cannock Chase. However, in the eleventh century this huge wooded tract was the property of kings - and only kings could own a forest. When the forest was sold to the Bishop of Lichfield in 1290, it became a chase.

The pious crocodiles of three black-clad Benedictine monks - a tall one, a thin one and a fat one, proceeding joyously towards their jewelled foundation crosses, portrays the continuing growth in the monastic movement during this century. Tutbury Priory was built by Henry de

Ferrers, a member of the new Norman nobility that the conquering King William thrust upon his Saxon subjects.

The story behind the monastery at Lapley takes us back to pre-conquest days when the Earls of Mercia were such a strong and influential family. In 1061, Burchard, the brother of Edwin and Morcar who were mentioned earlier, became gravely ill while travelling through France. He was cared for by the monks at the Abbey of St Regimus at Rheims. After his death, Birchard's father gave them land at Lapley in memory of the attention they had given to his dying son. Later in the century these foreign monks established a cell on their righteously acquired Lapley soil.

And so we come to the closing cameo on the panel, Halley's glittering Comet leaping through a silver crescent moon.

The comet can be seen from Earth at intervals of seventy-five years and it put in an appearance on 24th April 1066 when Harold, who had been King for less than four months, was already concerned with the threat of invasion from Duke William of Normandy. On the Bayeux Tapestry, the comet is depicted with an astrologer warning King Harold that it is an omen of ill fortune - and for Harold it was, for he was dead five months later.

Early medieval scribes had a penchant for decorating their maps and manuscripts with smiling suns and profile moons. Sylvia's moon is here in that context - simply as a decoration, closing the first century of the new millennium on an estimated ten thousand Norman aristocrats, lording it over a conquered Saxon population of between one and two million souls - very few of whom lived in devastated Staffordshire.

The Closing Motif

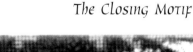

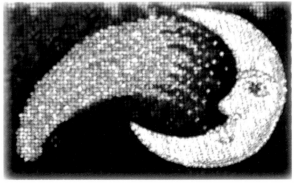

The Eleventh Century Embroidery Details

The padded sun was my first attempt at quilting leather. At this time I had not discovered leather needles, so it was very rough on my fingers, poking an ordinary needle through canvas, quilting, fixative and leather. Remember that there was only one chance at poking the needle through this great wodge of material - if I had not got it in the right place the sun would have come out sneering instead of smiling.

With only one exception, the central scene of each panel was worked directly onto the 12 count canvas, relying on a variety of stitches, usually tent stitch, but anything that helped me to depict exactly what I wanted to portray.

The Twelfth Century Embroidery Details

I loved working this panel. The background of mellow yellows and golds, in which the cameos are set, was easy on my eyes.

The intricacies of the gold leather lion was most time consuming. I had to create his features from a padded leather blank. I used padding to bring his rib cage into relief, and also to accentuate the muscles in his haunches. His claws and mane were created by couching with gold braid. The thinness of his long tail made this particularly difficult to handle.

To achieve a three dimensional effect I always envisage where the light is coming from as I embroider the picture. For instance, with the 'religious foundations' motif, I portrayed light coming from the left and reflecting off the columns. On Tamworth Castle, you will see that the light is coming from the opposite side.

The Twelfth Century

AD1100 Henry I Stephen Matilda Empress MIDLAND BANK HEDNESFORD Stephen

Roger Marmion receives Tamworth from Henry I

Tamworth

Stone + Eanwell 1140 Rocester + Radmore 1145
Ranton + Trentham 1150 + Stafford St Thomas 1174
Calwich + Sandwell 1180

de Toni Lord of Stafford

Market Charter
Lichfield 1149
Eccleshall 1149
Burton 1200
Newcastle

Lichfield Bower

Knights Templar Keele

Blackladies Brewood 1140
Farewell 1140 Brithbury 1140

Henry II Richard I AD1200

Cannock District Ladies

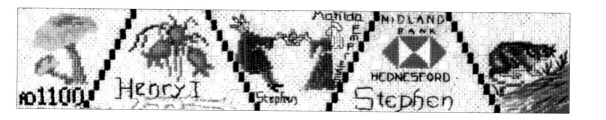

Kings and Queens of the Century

Henry I (Beauclerk and the Lion of Justice) reigned 1100-1135. William the Conqueror's fourth son. Married Edith (known as Matilda) and then Adela.

Stephen reigned 1135-1154. Nephew of Henry I. Married Matilda of Boulogne.

Henry II reigned 1154-1189. Grandson of Henry I by his daughter Matilda and Geoffrey Plantagenet. Married Eleanor of Aquitaine.

Richard I (Coeur-de-Lion) reigned 1189-1199. Son of Henry II. Married Berengaria of Navarre.

John reigned 1199-1216 Richard's brother. Married Isabelle, daughter of Earl of Gloucester, and then Isabelle of Angouleme.

Both William II, who was King in the first year of this century and Richard I, who was reigning in its final year, were killed by bowmen. Although there is no doubt that Richard's cross-bow bolt was meant for him, the debate goes on still as to whether King William was assassinated or the victim of a hunting companion's lousy shot.

The borders

The turn of the century brought in a new king and a big question mark over how his predecessor, William Rufus, had come to be shot in the chest with an arrow while out hunting. It was suggested that his younger brother Henry, who inherited the throne as Henry I, knew more about the accident than he was prepared to say.

King Henry had only two legitimate sons, William and Richard. Merry with drink and overconfident, William and his aristocratic young friends took the oars from the regular rowers on a sea crossing from Normandy to England and rowed themselves, Richard, a sister Maude and the whole contingent onto the Raz de Catteville rocks, and swift eternity.

Devastated at the loss of his sons and daughter, King Henry arranged a marriage between another daughter, Matilda, and Geoffrey of Anjou (Plantagenet). When Henry died, however, the Council, considering a woman unfit to rule, invited Matilda's cousin Stephen to be King. Sylvia's motif shows Stephen and Matilda quarrelling over the throne, plunging England into its first civil war of the millennium.

The Panel

The Opening Motif

When King Stephen's eldest son died in 1153 it paved the way for an end to the civil strife of the previous nineteen years. Stephen's second son had never expected to be King and seems not to have coveted the title, for an agreement was speedily reached between all relevant parties naming Matilda and Geoffrey Plantagenet's son, Henry, as heir apparent. This pact must have been a great relief to the people of Staffordshire who had been suffering the inconvenience and financial strain of hosting Henry's headquarters during his campaign against Stephen

The golden lion motif recognises Henry II's French connection through his father Geoffrey the Count of Anjou (Plantagenet). When Henry I married his daughter to Geoffrey, he presented his new son-in-law with a coat of arms, three red lions passant regardant, and these beasts have appeared on the royal coat of arms ever since.

Because of the ever constant threat of invasion from Scotland, Wales, Ireland and the Continent, William the Conqueror had, during the previous century, instructed his barons to either build or reinforce castles in the regions he granted to them. In return for their vast estates these lay lords were responsible for law and order, collecting taxes and providing the King with an army when the need arose, for in these medieval times a king could not afford to maintain a regular army himself.

When William was parceling up and sharing out England, he kept for himself the royal manors which had belonged to previous English Kings, such as Sedgley, Kingswinford and Penkridge. He also gave himself many of the manors that had belonged to the Earl of Mercia - Kinver, Uttoxeter and Leek for instance. Much of the rest of Mercia was divided between a few loyal followers including Henry de Ferrers, Robert Despenser, Robert de Toeni and William FitzAnsculf.

These lay lords, known as Barons, Lords, Earls or Dukes, owned so much land that it would have been impossible for them to work it themselves, and so they acted as tenants-in-chief, letting many of their manors (estates including the villages and hamlets) to their own relatives and followers.

King William had granted Tamworth including its Saxon fortress to Robert Despenser, and, when Robert died in 1114, a female relative, either a daughter or niece, who had married Robert Marmion, succeeded to the castle.

During the reign of King Henry I, Marmion fell out of favour for some obscure reason and his estates were confiscated by the Crown. However, after he died his son, Roger, fought on foreign soil for Henry and, as Sylvia's cameo shows, he was rewarded with the restoration of the family castle and estates. Much of the castle that you can visit today was the rebuilding work of another Robert Marmion who entertained King Henry II and Thomas a Becket there in 1157. The Marmion's enjoyed the tenure of their castle until the end of the thirteenth century when the male line again ran out and their properties passed through marriage to the Freville family.

Another of these fortune seeking Normans who grew rich on the spoils of the Conquest was Henry Ferrers. He was granted over two hundred manors, mostly in Derbyshire and Staffordshire, and he built his castle at Tutbury. These eleventh century feudal castles were not built of stone, but were after the French style of a defensive fort with a motte (earth mound) and bailey (courtyard) surrounded by a stockade made from split tree-trunks. They were the chief seat of the owner, from where he administered over his wide domain.

The dynasty that Henry Ferrers founded prospered and his son Robert was created Earl of Derby in 1138. However, the third Earl, William, joined a rebellion against King Henry II, and Tutbury Castle was besieged in 1174 and destroyed. Fortunately for the Ferrers dynasty though, the 6th Earl (another William) married the sister of his companion-in-arms Ranulph, Earl of Chester, and. when Ranulph died childless, William inherited, through his wife, Chartley Castle.

de Toni
Lord of Stafford

Roger de Toeni fought at the Battle of Hastings alongside William and so he and his family came in for rich pickings after the Conquest. Roger and Walter Giffard were William's two standard bearers and they both requested to be relieved of their duty at Hastings so that they could join in the affray. William consented, and Walter's descendant John Giffard has a story to tell about the battle, but I won't steal his thunder - we'll come to the Giffards in the fourteenth century.

When the Domesday book was compiled in 1086, telling William how much land there was in his new domain and exactly to whom he had given it all (and who he had pinched it from), Roger de Toeni's son, Robert, was shown to be the most landed lord in the Midlands, owning much of the property formerly belonging to Earl Edwin. As he had a cluster of estates around Stafford, Robert adopted the name de Stafford. It is probable that Robert built the first wooden, motte and bailey type castle at Stafford around 1070, as protection for his family and other Norman landowners, at that time still amongst a hostile, native Saxon community. However, the castle is not mentioned prior to a charter dated 1140, which could mean that it was built by a descendant of Robert during the dreadful strife of the Civil War in King Stephen's reign.

This century saw the foundation of a great many monastic establishments for both men and women.

Although a convent at Polesworth had survived a tenth century onslaught from the Danes, these ladies were later evicted from their abbey by Robert Marmion who wanted their land. Legend has it that his dreams were disturbed for the rest of his life because of this unchristian act, but, as he fell foul of King Henry I and lost his

Blackladies Brewood 1140
Farewell 1140 Blithbury 1140

lands anyway, there was little he could do to readdress the problem of the hapless nuns and secure himself a decent night's sleep. His grandson Robert Marmion reinstated the nuns at Polesworth, which stood him in good stead later when he was slain in a

Civil War skirmish. His body was carried to the abbey, but for some obscure reason, Robert was still under a Church ban and could not be buried in consecrated ground. However, the nuns, mindful of their benefactor's gracious act, received his remains and laid him to rest in a corner of the abbey orchard.

Three new Benedictine foundations were endowed for women in 1140 at Farewell near Lichfield, Blithbury and the Blackladies at Brewood.

There was a great deal of prestige to be gained from establishing a religious establishment and obviously, only the seriously wealthy could afford to do so because it was not simply a matter of erecting a fine building, the benefactor had also to endow the foundation with sufficient estates to enable it to be more or less self supporting.

Even so, there were a great many wealthy patrons eager to show their financial strength and importance, and a rash of new houses appeared - Stone, Canwell, Rocester, Radmore, Repton, Trentham, Stafford, St Thomas, Calwich and Sandwell are all examples of this twelfth century upsurge. To illustrate this monastic outbreak, Sylvia has added another monk to her pious crocodile, this time, as the going was getting easier, it's a fatter one.

The monks were industrious cultivators of the land and they turned their endowments - which were often poor scrub-land - into viable economic estates so that, by the end of this century, they were poised to become thirteenth century merchants and important landlords with considerable powers.

A preceptory of Knights Templars was formed under the patronage of Henry II in 1160 when the King gave them an estate at Keele. These monk-knights were the elite troops of the Christian army and later in the century fought alongside King Richard at the crusades. Sylvia has depicted her knight against the distinctive round towered church associated with their order, although there is no actual proof that such a building ever existed at Keele.

A fter the Norman Conquest no town was allowed to hold a market without obtaining a charter from the King, and these charters did not come cheaply. However, both the ecclesiastics and lay lords came to realise the benefits - to themselves - of encouraging outside trade to their manors and gradually began to obtain the necessary permission. The first of these charters granted in the County were to Lichfield and Eccleshall in 1149, although there is no known date for Newcastle-under-Lyme's charter so it may have been earlier.

With a charter in place, the Lord of the Manor could set up his formal trading area and charge rents to the traders for the right to gather there and sell their wares in a "publicly exposed, fixed place". This "publicly exposed, fixed place" was either the green outside the church, the road through the centre of the village, or the place in the village where two or more roads crossed. Wherever it was, the market cross went with it. These early merchants could neither read nor write and so they had to have some easy, generally understood form of agreement, and a handshake in front of the market cross became the forerunner to a signature on a piece of paper.

Once the charter was purchased, the Lord's income did not stop at the rental received from the market stalls; he was also permitted to collect tolls on goods entering the town, and taxes on goods sold, thus bringing in a considerable income if the market was successful and attracted plenty of traders.

A thriving market was good for everybody's trade. The merchants needed victuals and possibly lodgings for the night as well as somewhere to stable their pack-horses. The local farmers and craftsmen were encouraged to grow and produce saleable goods now that they had a guaranteed outlet for their wares, and the lord of the manor creamed a percentage off the top of it all.

T here is no certainty as to how long the people of Lichfield have been celebrating Whit Monday with the Greenhill Bower Festival. As with the Abbots Bromley Horn Dance (see 11th century), the festival has changed and adapted over the years so that it continues to appeal to the requirements of each successive generation and it probably bears scant resemblance to the rites performed eight hundred or more years ago. The day starts with the crowning of the Bower Queen and then a procession winds through the main streets of the City and ends at the Bower House erected for the occasion on Greenhill. One popular theory has its origins in the fact that King Henry II needed to know how many fighting men he could rely upon and how well equipped they might be to wage war for him (remember that there was no regular army at this time). To obtain this information, the City Fathers decreed that all men between the age of fifteen and sixty should gather on Greenhill so that a View of Arms could take place. After the ceremony a procession was formed to lead the men-at-arms back down to the Market Square where, now that the serious business was over and done with, everyone spent the rest of the day merrymaking.

Sylvia has shown the church of St Michael's nestled in the folds of Greenhill. The churchyard here is probably older even than the Greenhill Bower custom, as local lore tells that it was this ancient Saxon burial-ground that drew St Chad to choose Lichfield as the centre of his new diocese.

The Closing Motif

King Richard I reigned for ten years, although less than a year of that time was spent in England. His native tongue was French and he could neither write nor speak English. In fact, his only interest in England was in the funds it could provide for his crusades. He died during the last year of the century after a crossbow bolt hit him in the shoulder during a pathetically insignificant wrangle over a cache of treasure at the castle of Chalus in the Limousin. Richard wanted the treasure and besieged the castle against a garrison of no more than fifteen ill equipped soldiers. While he lay dying from his gangrenous wound, the castle was taken and the young crossbowman who had fired the fatal shot was brought to him. When the King asked what grievance the soldier held against him, the youth replied that his two brothers and his father had been killed by Richard's men and that he was pleased to see that Richard was mortally wounded. Apparently, without resentment Richard ordered the young man to be released, but the story goes that the soldiers detained him and after Richard's death he was flogged and then hanged.

The Thirteenth Century

ᴀᴅ1200 John Cacoeand Henry III

Magna Carta

Sir John de Weston

MARKET

Chartley Cattle

Abbots Bromley 1200
Market Charters – Cannock · Rugeley 1259
Penkridge 1244 Uttoxeter 1257

Seal of Stafford Borough

1203

1200 to 1300

Roger de Sommerville
Lord of Alrewas

Wool Exporting Abbeys
Croxden · Burton

Great Fire of Burton 1255

Lichfield Friary
1229

Dieu la Cres Abbey
1221

Households 1298
Cannock 90 Rugeley 90 Brewood
157

founded by
Ranulf of Chester

Edward I

the Scots

NEWCASTLE
UNDER · LYME
BOROUGH COUNCIL

ᴀᴅ1300

Kings and Queens of the Century

John (Lackland) reigned 1199-1216. Married Isabelle daughter of Earl of Gloucester and then Isabelle of Angouleme.

Henry III reigned 1216-1272. Married Eleanor of Provence.

Edward I (Longshanks) 1272-1307. Married Eleanor of Castile.

The borders

King John was the youngest of Henry II's four sons and so his chances of inheriting anything of significance were remote. It is said that it was King Henry himself who dubbed the infant John 'Lackland'. However in 1189 when John was twenty-two and his father died, two of his brothers, Henry and Geoffrey, were already dead, and the new King, Richard, was a homosexual with such a lack of interest in his neglected young wife, Berengaria, that it was unlikely she would produce heirs. Richard was killed in 1199 and John, now thirty two years old, became King.

Much later in the century, when Edward I was King, his ambition was to rule over an undivided nation of England, Scotland and Wales. He managed to bring the Welsh into line and so in 1301 he created Edward, one of his sons, Prince of Wales, a title since borne by all male heirs to the throne. Scotland steadfastly refused to be subdued although the King waged war on them relentlessly. His tomb in Westminster Abbey bears the legend "Here lies Edward the Hammer of the Scots."

The Panel

The Opening Motif

The flamboyant, crusading King Richard must have been a tough act to follow and his brother John has gone down in history as an unpleasant, cruel and avaricious man, who probably had something to do with the murder of his young nephew Arthur of Brittany, because of the boy's strong claim to the throne.

In 1215 some of John's barons rebelled against him and on the island of Runnymede, in the River Thames near Windsor, he was forced to sign a charter defining royal powers, baronial rights and the liberties of his subjects. Not all of the barons were involved in this rebellion and both William de Ferrers, whose forbears appear in the twelfth century panel, and his brother-in-law, Ranulph, Earl of Chester, remained loyal to John throughout his life and were close enough allies to act as witnesses to his death-bed will.

The charter was amended several times after John's death the following year, and at the time of the 1217 amendment, another smaller charter, dealing with the forest laws, was also issued. To avoid confusion, King John's charter became known as the Magna Carta (large charter).

To keep the Danes out of Mercia, Ethelfleda, the Lady of Mercia, built fortresses at Tamworth and Stafford in the year 913. However, the realm had been weakened by the long years of Viking onslaughts and when Ethelfleda died five years later, the kingdom of Mercia submitted to the rule of King Edward of Wessex.

It is perhaps around this time that Edward's·'Wessex' form of administration was introduced into Mercia and the territory divided into five shires, each based on a fortified town, Leicestershire, Derbyshire, Warwickshire, Worcestershire and Staffordshire. All this is theory because there is no actual record that this is when the county of Staffordshire came into existence, in fact, its first mention is not until a hundred years later in 1016.

Although Stafford was a young settlement and situated in marshland, it seems to have been chosen as the shire town because it was more central than Chester or Shrewsbury, and Tamworth may have been considered too near the other county towns of Leicester, Derby and Warwick.

In the reign of Edward the Confessor (1042-1066) the town paid £6 tax a year to the Crown and £3 to Edwin the Earl of Mercia, but in 1086 Edwin's share had been annexed by King William and the total tax assessment was reduced to £7. This makes Stafford the only town which paid less tax after the Conquest than before. This state of affairs was the result of William's harsh treatment of the area after the 1069/70 rebellions, and Domesday, compiled twenty years after the harrying, recorded that fifty-one of the town's 128 houses were 'waste'.

With such a small population base, recovery was very slow indeed and it took several generations before Stafford thrived again. However in 1206, King John issued a charter to the town conferring on it the status of a free borough and as this document seems to have been more or less dotting the 'i's and crossing the 't's of an existing situation, Stafford must have been well on its feet by the beginning of this century.

Although most of the townspeople were completely unable to read or write they were gradually being made aware of their community responsibilities and the burgesses - the literate, chief citizens of the borough from whom the town councillors were elected - were generating important, legally binding documentation. Sylvia has depicted the borough's common seal as her central motif, indicating the sophisticated degree of local government that was now developing.

As the County pulled itself together after William the Conqueror's merciless attentions and the population steadily increased, so the scrubland and woods were cleared to make way for crop growing, sheep farming and housing.

With more mouths to feed and more bodies to clothe, there was a greater requirement for people to be able to buy and sell, and so the lay lords and the clergy clamoured to the King for market charters so that they could attract traders to their villages - and enhance their personal wealth out of the stall rents, taxes and tolls that they could charge.

Leek received a charter as early as 1208. Some entirely new settlements were created, such as Uttoxeter, where in 1252 the Ferrers family laid out over a hundred plots of land for rent and some thirty market stalls. The plots or tenements attracted freemen to come and live in the town, and these people were the very sort that became involved in community affairs and local government.

Henry III, during his long reign, granted twenty Staffordshire towns and villages a weekly market and an annual fair. Applications were not automatically sanctioned though, because as a general rule a charter would be refused where a market already existed within a six mile radius.

Sylvia shows the increase in husbandry and trading where the farmer and his family, laden down with home grown produce herd their livestock in the direction of a distant market cross. Even the small boy does his share, carrying a piglet. (Sylvia is very proud of this piglet which she created in a tiny space with a minimum of stitches).

Obtaining the coveted market charter was usually the first step towards turning a small settlement into a flourishing town and Sylvia's thriving late thirteenth century village is all set up, ready to surge ahead on the wave of prosperity that embraced this and the next century. There is a watermill, a blacksmith's forge, the tithe barn and church, some cottages around a village green, a duck pond complete with its wildlife, the market cross signifying that a weekly market took place, and a well stocked sheep fold. Yet such a village did not automatically become an urban sprawl, as the population figures of 1298 show - Cannock and Rugeley, now huge twentieth century conurbations, supported just ninety households apiece seven hundred years ago, while Brewood, today a rural backwater jostling for the Best Kept Village award, enjoyed the affluence derived from a religious foundation on its doorstep, and boasted 157 families.

STOP PRESS
Extract from Express and Star - 10th August 1999
Residents in Brewood were celebrating today after winning their category in the 1999 Staffordshire Best Kept Village awards, and going through to the national finals. The village first won the Express & Star trophy for the Best Kept Village South Staffordshire District last night and was then declared the Best Large Village in the whole of the County. It was also nominated for the National Village of the Year Award.

The Best Kept Village awards were made at a presentation ceremony at Weston Village Hall - which brings me to Sir John de Weston. By this century, the villages and estates of Newton and Weston, which had been confiscated from their Saxon owner at the time of the conquest, were owned by Sir Hamo de Weston and Newton who died in 1214 leaving his lands to his son Sir John de Weston. Later in the century, John's grandson Sir Hugh exchanged land in Newton belonging to St Thomas' Priory

for land in Weston-under-Lizard and henceforth the de Westons lived at Weston rather than at Newton. The male line petered out several times over the centuries and it was in fact a female descendant's marriage with the Lord of the Manor of Walsall which ultimately brought the Earls of Bradford to Weston Park.

In 1203 King John granted the Manor of Alrewas to Roger de Sommerville. Sylvia describes Roger as the archetypal civil servant, for he and his descendants wrote down everything that happened on the Alrewas patch, giving historians an abundance of useful information, facts and fugures. As most of Roger's contemporaries and their lineage did not have this inclination for 'number crunching', the Alrewas statistics are, in many instances, all that the County has to go on. Thank you, Roger de Sommerville - Sylvia salutes you and has placed your shield here on the thirteenth century panel as a tribute to your industrious jottings.

The growth of villages and towns with the gathering together of people in close proximity had its problems as well as its benefits.

The lack of sanitation brought disease, and the houses, which were mainly wattle and daub with thatched roofs, presented a constant fire hazard. The village of Stone burnt

down in 1264 and both Lichfield and Leek went up in flames in the 1290s. The conflagration at Leek was so fierce that even the stone-built St Edward's church had to be rebuilt. In 1255, the 'Great Fire of Burton' - which nobody seems to have heard of - destroyed all but the church tower and the town's long, multi-arched bridge over the Trent. The bridge survived to witness history for another six centuries until 1864 when the new thirty two arched structure was built to replace it.

Some of the monasteries which were shown to be consolidating their wealth in the twelfth century were now hugely powerful institutions. Although the lands with which they had started were usually poor, bleak and exposed, a hundred or so years of husbandry had turned them into rich pastures where sheep and cows thrived. So these monks-cum-merchants were now running lucrative sheep farms and exporting wool. There were small enterprises such as the Knights Templar at Keele with about 200 sheep, but also there were the heavy-weights such as the Benedictines at Burton with

6,000 sheep plus a substantial cattle herd. The Cistercians at Croxden, founded in 1176 and so relatively new to the County, had over 7,200 sheep grazing on the north-east moorlands.

There is an interesting claim made by the folk of Croxden that is duplicated by the people of Croxton in Leicestershire. In 1215 and 1216 King John was getting trouble from two-thirds of his barons who had thrown in their lot with Prince Louis of France upholding his claim to be rightful King of England. This claim was based on the fact that his wife was the grand-daughter of King Henry II and sister of the murdered, young Arthur of Brittany. John spent long months dashing about his kingdom putting down rebellions until, in the early autumn of 1216, he became sick with dysentery. In October he arrived at Newark Castle, still ill and with the added distress of having lost his treasure in the quicksands of the Wash. There, tended by the Abbot of Croxden he died. Although his body was interred in Worcester Cathedral in accordance with John's wishes, the story goes that the Abbot took out the King's heart and carried it away to be buried in Croxden Abbey. And there lies the dispute; was it Croxton Abbey, or Croxden Abbey here in Staffordshire?

When I called at Sylvia's house one day shortly after starting the book, I found to my dismay the cameo of the badge of Sir William Wastneys, Lord of Colton, abandoned on the floor, and a new vignette being appliquéd on to the panel. I was quite unaware that this was going to happen time and again! As Sylvia worked on the panels, she quite happily snipped out hours of intricate embroidery to include some other idea that had taken her fancy, or made a more interesting historical pattern. So if you have one of the very early postcards, you won't have the Dieulacres abbey.

As with Croxden, fable surrounds the Cistercian abbey of Dieulacres near Leek. It was founded in 1214 by Ranulph the 6th Earl of Chester (he who was to witness King John's will), reputedly on account of a dream. During King Stephen's reign, the Earl of Chester (Ranulph's grandfather) had founded an abbey at Poulton in Cheshire, which was now being subjected to the unwanted attentions of the Welsh and failing to flourish. Ranulph told his wife that the old Earl had appeared to him in a dream instructing him to move the Cistercian monks to a safer, more favourable place. 'Dieu encres' - may God grant it increase - his wife replied, and so, the new abbey became known as Dieulacres. Notice that the monk in this vignette is dressed in a white robe - Cistercian monks wore white, whereas the earlier foundations in Staffordshire were Benedictine and wore black robes.

The only information that Sylvia had to go on when it came to re-creating the Lichfield friary was the fact that King Henry III had assigned the friars ten oak trees, from each of the hays (animal enclosures) of Alrewas, Bentley and Hopwas in Cannock Forest, with which to build their chapel and dwellings. Later he doubled the consignment from Alrewas when the friars informed him that Hopwas Hay did not have suitable timber for their purposes.

Such scant available knowledge gave plenty of room for artistic licence and so we have here Lichfield's Franciscan friary - a house of mobile preachers, à la Sylvia. What we do know is that the friary was a victim of commercial enterprise at the time of Henry VIII's Act of Dissolution when a consortium of local townsmen bought the building for £46 so that they could demolish it and take away the materials for resale.

At the time of the Conquest, Staffordshire supported freely roaming herds of pure white cattle, well protected by the harsh forest laws which precluded them, along with the deer and wild boar, from being hunted by the local population. These animals, with black ears and branching horns were probably descended from primitive English aurochs which the Romans had domesticated during their occupation here. It seems that William Ferrers, Earl of Derby (yes, the other witness to King John's will), who had inherited Chartley Castle and estates when his brother-in-law, the Earl of Chester, died, drove a herd of these fearsome creatures from Needwood Forest into the great park at Chartley to save them from being hunted to extinction once the forest laws were relaxed. There the herd, about 45 strong in the late nineteenth century, remained until in-breeding and tuberculosis reduced their number to eleven, including a very rare black heifer.

At this time the Ferrers parted with their Chartley estate and the remnants of the herd were, fortunately, offered a home by the Duke of Bedford at Woburn, where they remained for some years whilst a concerted effort to save them from extinction was mounted. At about the same time that William Ferrers had rounded up his cattle at Chartley, four other herds were also driven into manorial parks throughout the country. The Chillingham herd of Northumberland and the Vaynol herd of North Wales still exist as separate breeds, but the Chartley, Cadzow and Dynevor herds were so depleted, their survival could only be secured by pooling them to form the White Park breed.

The Cotswold Farm Park near Stow-on-the-Wold, Cheltenham, established their own herd of these White Park Cattle in 1969 and called it the 'Bemborough'. It has been a very successful venture and animals born to this new herd have taken the Championship at the Rare Breeds National Show on several occasions.

Sylvia uses the fleur de lys here to symbolise the first time an English King had set his sights on the French crown. Considering the problems Edward I was having with the Scots, who refused to be 'hammered', and his barons, who were, as ever, reluctant to pay taxes, it might have been reasonable for him to leave France alone. But the King upset his barons and religious magnates yet again by taxing their wool trade to fund an invasion of France in September 1197. The military campaign was inconclusive and a disappointed Edward formed a truce with King Philip IV of France. To cement relations, Edward, white haired and sixty, married the seventeen year old sister of the French King, and, to the King's eight year old daughter, betrothed his son, Edward of Caernarvon.

The Closing Motif

The Thirteenth Century Embroidery Details

As you can see, I normally worked the opening motif in gold or silver leather, but for the Magna carta scroll I used gold tissue because I wanted to give the supple effect of parchment and I felt that leather would look too rigid.

The pig in my 'family goes to market' scene is a little gem; he consists of no more than a couple of dozen stitches, and I am sure you'll agree, he looks remarkably porcine.

The "households population' scene was another very busy cameo worked on 24 count canvas. It took me two weeks to design and embroider this scene.

The Fourteenth Century Embroidery Details

Do not embroider onto a red background unless you really have to, it is very tiring on the eyes. I loved doing the strap work on all the panels, and this one, I think, is my favourite.

The cathedral is embroidered directly onto the 12 count canvas which does not give a great deal of definition, so I was very pleased with the amount of architectural and three dimensional detail I managed to capture.

This was the first panel on which I unpicked and replaced a cameo. Original postcards show a famine scene whereas the final panel shows the Whittington Manor.

Several people have asked me for the motifs I have taken off, but unpicking is a destructive process and reduces the cameos to tatters.

The Fourteenth Century

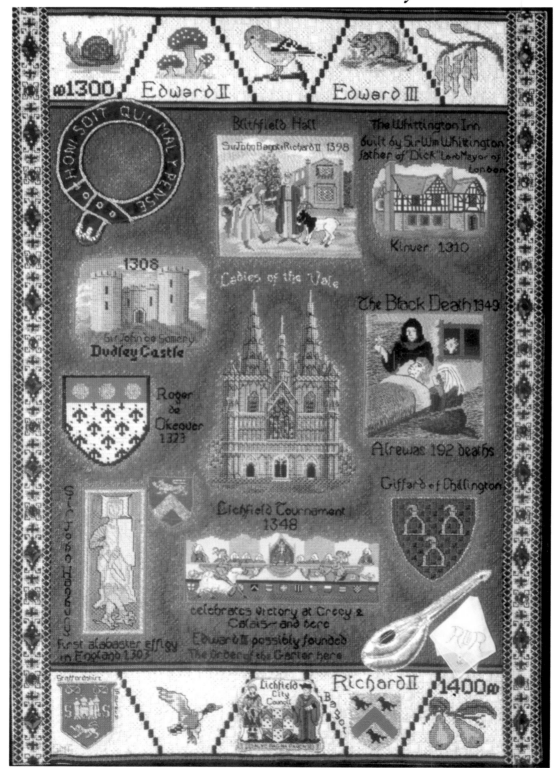

ω1300 Edward II Edward III

HONI SOIT QUI MAL Y PENSE

Blithfield Hall
Sir John Bagot Richard II 1398

The Whittington Inn
Built by Sir Wm Whittington
father of "Dick" Lord Mayor of
London

Kinver 1310

1308
Sir John de Somery
Dudley Castle

Ladies of the Vale

The Black Death 1349

Roger
de
Okeover
1323

Alrewas 192 deaths

Giffard of Chillington

Sir John Hastang

Lichfield Tournament
1348

celebrates victory at Crecy &
Calais — and here
Edward III possibly founded
The Order of the Garter here

first alabaster effigy
in England 1303

RUR

Staffordshire

Lichfield
City
Council

Bagot

Richard II 1400 ω

Kings and Queens of the century

Edward II reigned 1307-1327. The first Prince of Wales. Married Isabel of France. He was forced to abdicate in favour of his grandson and then murdered.

Edward III reigned 1327-1377. Married at the age of sixteen to Philippa of Hainault, age fourteen. Their son was Edward the Black Prince who died in 1376.

Richard II reigned 1377-1399. Son of the Black Prince, he was ten years old when he acceded to the throne on the death of his grandfather. He was forced to abdicate and the crown was seized by his cousin Henry IV - another grandson of Edward III.

As with the eleventh century, the thirteenth began and ended with a king who came to a questionable end. Edward II in 1327 and Richard II in 1399 were both forced from their thrones and then met unnatural deaths.

The Panel

The Opening Motif

The reign of Edward III saw the start of the Hundred Years War with France and when the King and his nobles returned in triumph from Crecy and Calais a round of celebratory festivities were held throughout the country.

These jubilations, which became known as the 'round table tournaments' re-enacted the story of King Arthur's chivalrous deeds and occasionally ended with some seriously injured noblemen, as the knights, and even the King, jousted in front of splendidly bedecked courtiers and other privileged hangers on.

This 'round table' concept, in which the King accepted the chivalrous equality of a select band of knights, was eventually formalised into the founding of the Order of the Knights of the Garter.

At Lichfield we have one of the smallest medieval cathedrals in England and it stands on one of the earliest English sites of a Christian church.

Christianity first came to Staffordshire in AD653 when the King of Mercia married a Christian princess from Northumbria and brought her back to his kingdom, along with four missionaries who were to convert his subjects to the new religion. Chad, a Northumbrian monk came along sixteen years later in 669 when he was appointed the first Bishop of Mercia. He established his See at Lichfield where he lived and worked for just three years until he died of the plague in 672. Sylvia chose this century to depict the cathedral because it was during the late thirteenth and early fourteenth centuries that much

of the building we know today, including the three spires (known affectionately as the Ladies of the Vale) finally emerged from the earlier Norman structure.

More damage was done to Lichfield Cathedral than to any other cathedral during the Civil War of the seventeenth century. As a result of systematic bombardment by the Parliamentarians the building was virtually roofless for fifteen years until Bishop Hackett raised the funds to start restoration work in about 1662.

Sadly, the toxic atmosphere of our own century is wreaking another bombardment upon the Cathedral, slowly eating away at the one hundred and thirteen 19th century statues carved into the world famous west front of the building. Indeed, the stone masons seem to be fighting a losing battle in their attempts to restore eroded carvings and other stone work in every quarter of the building, so please don't forget to feed some coins into the glass fronted box which begs for your donation and explains that it costs £2000 a day to maintain our beautiful cathedral.

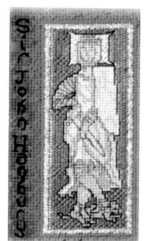

Little is known of the deeds of Sir John Hanbury. His claim to fame lies not in his accomplishments in this life which ended in 1303, but in the material of his effigy in the church at Hanbury. Sir John, his legs crossed in the manner which usually denotes the calling of a Crusader, is beautifully crafted in alabaster - doubtless the work of a local carver. By the end of the century Hanbury and the surrounding area enjoyed a healthy industry in the supply of alabaster and when Edward III's son, John of Gaunt, required a tomb for his wife, he had two large blocks sent to London from his own Tutbury pits.

And Sir John is not Hanbury's only claim to fame. Legend has it that Chester Cathedral owes its very existence to this small village. Around the middle of the seventh century St Werburgh, the daughter of Wulfhere, the Saxon King of Mercia, founded a nunnery at Hanbury and another at Trentham. She made it known that when she died she wished to be buried at Hanbury and ultimately, after a little unpleasantness with the nuns at Trentham who had interred her in their own abbey, she came 'home' to rest. Not, however for long. About 170 years later, the marauding Danes, lacking both Christianity and culture, were a real threat of desecration to Werburgh's remains, and the nuns fled with her relics to Chester. The cathedral, which is dedicated to her, was begun as her shrine.

By no means all of the families who jumped on to Duke William's fortune-seeking bandwagon have survived the centuries. As mentioned in the map panel, the Ansculfs of Dudley Castle were there but fleetingly. The Paganels who followed them were not much more successful at founding a dynasty either, and within a hundred years John de Somery obtained a neglected, unfortified castle, by marrying the surviving female Paganel heir.

The de Somery's prospered and were allowed to re-fortify the castle after its slighting in the time of Gervaise Paganel, and, in 1306, John de Somery was knighted. His unchivalrous behaviour would certainly not have merited his entry into King Edward III's elite Order of the Garter - but Edward was only a boy when John was running his medieval protection racket, forcing his local tenant farmers to either pay him cash or assist in the rebuilding of his castle. He left no heirs when he died in 1321 and so the Castle changed hands yet again, this time to his sister's husband, John de Sutton. It remained with that family - who changed their name to Dudley - for the next 400 years, during which time one rather obscure offshoot of the clan produced star performers in many a Tudor intrigue.

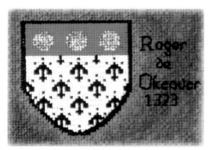

When surnames became necessary the Okeovers of Okeover in Dovedale adopted the name of their manor. This family boasted a strong claim to a pre-conquest pedigree as records show that round about the turn of the eleventh century the monks of Burton Abbey granted the manor of Okeover to a tenant by the name of Orm. Now this Orm appears to have been the son of the previous tenant Eddulf and as both of these names are Saxon it would indicate that we have here a family who survived William the Conqueror's redistribution of the land. Orm was a direct ancestor of the Okeovers and, really, the family owe their fame to nothing other than just quietly being there, century after century after century, passing their manor down through the male line right up until Haughton Ealdred Okeover's death in 1955.

The Bagots of Blithfield Hall are another landed family in the County who do not owe their beginnings to William the Conqueror - they can boast that they were here before him. How they managed to hang on, when most other Saxon thanes suffered the confiscation of their estates, remains an intriguing mystery. Unlike the Okeovers, the Bagots did not keep their heads down and quietly live their lives in rural seclusion. Throughout medieval times there isn't a century of our Staffordshire history when a Bagot or two doesn't crop up mixing and marrying amongst the Norman

elite and, as Sylvia's vignette shows, even 'hob-nobbing' with the King himself.

The legend goes that King Richard II, delighted with the hunting he had enjoyed in Sir John Bagot's park, presented his host with a herd of goats brought back from the

Crusades. They were residents at the park until earlier this century.

When Sylvia visited the current Lady Bagot to authenticate the ancient shield shown in the bottom border, she asked too, whether there was any truth in the famous tale of how the goats were originally acquired. 'Well, it's a nice story', was as far as Lady Bagot would be drawn on the subject, and so Sylvia has shown Sir John making his obeisance to his King, Richard II, in front of the Hall, his hand resting casually on the head of one of his goats. 'Draw your own conclusion', Sylvia suggests.

On the other hand, the Giffards of Chillington Hall are a family who do, most certainly, owe their stake in England to William the Conqueror. According to the current owner of Chillington Hall, John Giffard, his distant forebear Walter de Giffard crossed the Channel with Duke William of Normandy, as one of his two standard bearers (hence the three stirrups on the Giffard coat of arms - the extra one is for the standard). Giffard legend also asserts that it was an arrow from Walter's bow which killed Harold, a fact confirmed, they say by an inscription on the Bayeux Tapestry. Well, to quote Lady Bagot, 'it's a nice story' and if I were a Giffard I am sure I would believe it - but I can't find anything written down anywhere that confirms this account of Walter's prowess as an archer, so I am hiding behind Sylvia's advice here and asking you to draw your own conclusion.

There are many stories surrounding the occasion on which King Edward III founded the Order of the Knights of the Garter. Some historians suggest that it was at Windsor in 1348, at a tournament celebrating the purification of his Queen, Philippa, after the birth of the fourth of her twelve children. Then there's the story of a beautiful courtesan's blue garter which Edward is supposed to have picked up at a ball held to celebrate the fall of Calais. The Royal Household accounts record that a new bed was ordered for the King at that time, specifying a decoration of blue taffeta, powdered with the garter emblems and the motto 'Honi soit qui mal y pense' - evil be to him who evil thinks.

One of the spectacular tournaments, held to celebrate the battles of Crècy and Calais, was held outside the Cathedral at Lichfield in April 1348, and the fact that twenty six of the founder knights of the Order of the Garter were present at this gathering has lead several historians to suggest that this was when Edward founded the Order. As the original statutes are lost, nobody knows for sure, and so Sylvia, ever keen to capture a little glory for her native Staffordshire has taken this theory on board.

At about the time that King Edward and his knights were jousting their way round the country celebrating the success of their French campaigns, a sinister visitor slipped quietly into England via rat-infested ships. The Black Death spread into Staffordshire in the Spring of 1349 and thanks to the descendants of Roger de Sommerville, (see the 13th century) who were still taking great care to record the comings and goings in their Manor, we learn that the plague's death toll in Alrewas was May - 60, June - 70, July - 50, and that, by the time the disease had run its course, 192 people had died. For full effect, these figures need to be compared with the normal death rate in the village which was two or three a month. We can assume that all over Staffordshire similar losses were suffered.

It is estimated that this visitation of the plague depleted the population of England by a third, an utterly devastating statistic in terms of human suffering. However, looking at this ravaging of the workforce from a purely material point of view, it was by no means all doom and gloom for the survivors. As villages became deserted, farm buildings decayed and arable land became pasture for want of labour, the peasant, for the first time, became worthy of his hire. At Pattingham, tenants taking over uncultivated land or agreeing to repair dilapidated buildings were waived entry tolls.

The plague returned briefly to Staffordshire in 1361, reducing again the workforce, and by the end of the century tenants had enough muscle to refuse to perform the labour owed to their lord, and enough money to offer him cash in lieu of ploughing, mowing and haymaking on the Manor farm. Never again was the Staffordshire peasant as down-trodden and impoverished as he had been in the pre-plague era.

The next vignette was a late comer to the panel. Any reader who possesses one of the original post-cards printed before Sylvia decided that she couldn't ignore the Whittington Manor House at Kinver, will find a different motif directly above the Black Death scene. Having already written about the famine scene originally depicted, I groused when I saw the 14th century panel back on the frame and the new

scene being worked. 'Well, I couldn't ignore Whittington Manor House, could I?' Sylvia pouted, 'after all, it's not every county that has its own Pantomime character!'

Sir William de Whittington owned the whole of Kinver where he built his oak-framed manor house in 1310. William was the grandfather of Dick Whittington, Lord Mayor of London, and this being the case, it rather belies the tale that young Dick was a poor youth when he set off to make his fortune!

The manor house was sold in 1352 to Thomas de Lowe and it was his great-grand-daughter who married into the Grey family thus bringing the property ultimately to the uncle of Lady Jane Grey who became Queen for nine days. The tragic young Jane spent part of her childhood in her uncle's care at the manor house and there are rumours of her haunting one of the staircases there. Later, the house is said to have played host to King Charles II as he made his way across the County after the battle of Worcester. Then, in 1711, Queen Anne was a guest for the night during one of her Royal Progresses and the front door still bears her iron seal as witness to the event. The property became an Inn during the eighteenth century and today still trades as The Whittington Inn.

The Closing Motif

In 1399, Richard II the last Plantagenet king was forced to abdicate. One of Richard's greatest problems seems to have been that his grandfather was over fecund. Edward III had five sons and a clutch of daughters, most of whom married and reproduced so that Richard had any amount of cousins with reasonable claims to his crown. His uncle, John of Gaunt, and his son, Henry, who seized the throne, set the course for civil turmoil during the next century, when several other descendants of Edward III schemed to be King of England.

Basically, Richard hadn't the stomach for the job of medieval king. He was less inclined to use his court as a war-office than as a base for promoting music, poetry and fashion - apparently, we owe to him the invention of the pocket handkerchief.

The Fifteenth Century

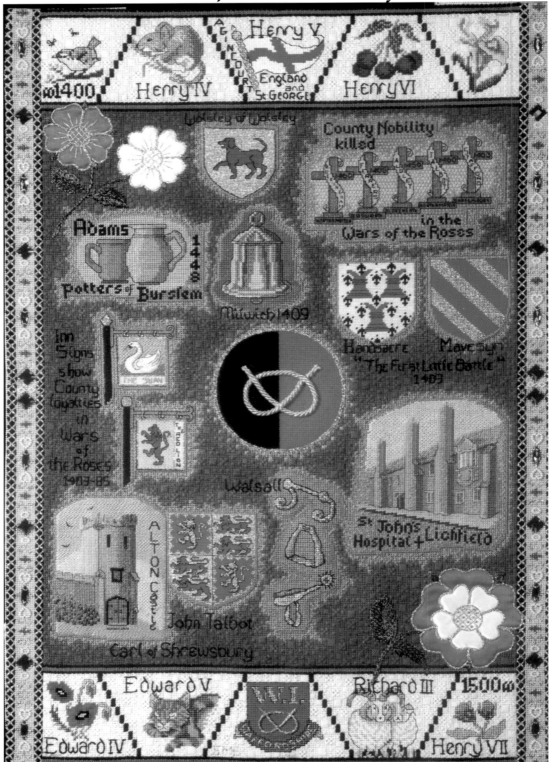

ɷ1400   Henry IV   AGINCOURT   Henry V   England and St George   Henry VI

Wolseley of Wolseley

County Nobility killed ... in the Wars of the Roses

Abams 1448   Potters of Burslem

Milwich 1409

Inn Signs show County loyalties in Wars of the Roses 1403-85

THE SWAN

STAFFORD

Hanbacre   Mavesyn "The First Little Battle" 1403

Walsall

St John's Hospital Lichfield

ALTON Castle   John Talbot   Earl of Shrewsbury

Edward IV   Edward V   W.I. STAFFORD   Richard III   1500ɷ   Henry VII

Kings and Queens of the Century

Henry IV reigned 1399-1413. The first King of the House of Lancaster. Henry was the son of John of Gaunt the Duke of Lancaster, and a grandson of Edward III.

Henry V reigned 1413-1422. Married Katherine of Valois, daughter of Charles VI, the mad King of France. Henry died suddenly aged 35 - had he lived two weeks longer he would have been King of France.

Henry VI reigned 1422-1461 and 1470-71. Married Margaret of Anjou. The last king of the House of Lancaster. He suffered from occasional fits of madness inherited from his French mother. He was murdered in 1471.

Edward IV. The first Yorkist king. He seized the crown and reigned 1461-1470 and 1471-1483. In 1464 he secretly married Elizabeth Woodville who was a widow with two sons. This was a love-match, at least on Edward's side, and ruffled the feathers of his advisers no end because they were planning to marry him to a French princess.

Edward V. This twelve year old son of Edward IV was never crowned. He was King from 9th April to 25th June 1483. Along with his nine year old brother, the young Edward V disappeared after being taken, ostensibly for safety reasons, to live in the Tower of London. During alterations at the Tower in 1674 the skeletons of two children were discovered and subsequently acknowledged as King Edward V and his brother (the Princes in the Tower).

Richard III (Crookback) reigned 1483-1485. Married Anne Neville. The last king of the House of York, he died at the battle of Bosworth. He may have been a thoroughly bad lot, but he can at least help you to remember the colours of the rainbow: Richard Of York Gave Battle In Vain - red, orange, yellow, green, blue, indigo, violet.

Henry VII reigned 1485-1509. The first Tudor monarch. He was a Lancastrian. His marriage to Elizabeth of York linked the two families ending the 'Wars of the Roses'.

The borders

The Bard, not normally known for his links with Staffordshire gets a look-in, albeit a century early, when Sylvia links him to Henry V and his Agincourt battlecry, *"God for Harry, England and St George."*

Not in the borders, but this seems the right time to mention the oldest dated bell in Staffordshire, hanging in Milwich church tower since 1409. When news of King Henry's victory at Agincourt eventually filtered through to Staffordshire, the chimes from this bell would have told the villagers and the surrounding districts of the good news.

The Panel

The Opening Motif

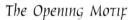

Two roses growing from the same stem - the red rose for the House of Lancaster and the white rose for the House of York - are symbolic of the struggle for power between the descendants of King Edward III's power-seeking brood. The struggle for the throne, often referred to as 'the cousins' wars', spanned two centuries and affected the reigns of seven kings from Richard II, who was forced to abdicate in favour of his cousin Henry IV in 1399, to Henry VII, who won the crown in 1485.

The Staffords, descendants of one of William the Conqueror's standard bearers, Roger de Toeni, had been doing rather well for themselves over the centuries and had risen through the hierarchy to become earls. There had been several excellent marriages which had brought more wealth and splendid property into the family, so their original castle at Stafford was now only one of many residences in their possession.

Most prestigious of the marriages was in the previous century when Edmund, the 5th Earl, married a grand-daughter of Edward III, linking the Staffords with royalty. It seems that it may have been at about this time that the family started to use the Stafford knot as a heraldic badge - or to use a modern term 'logo'. There is no doubt that the Stafford knot emblem was originally worn on the livery of the Stafford family, but somewhere along the line it was adopted by both the Borough and the County of Stafford so that it has become known, quite erroneously as the Stafford*shire* knot.

The Staffords were Lancastrians, supporting King Henry IV's snatching of the throne, and their support stood them in good stead because during the century Humphrey Stafford was created Duke of Buckingham.

Another royal match came the way of this ambitious family when Henry, the 2nd Duke of Buckingham, married Catherine Woodville who was King Edward IV's sister-in-law. By now, without doubt, the Staffords were one of the best connected families in England.

But in April 1483 the Duke of Buckingham deserted the Lancastrian cause and masterminded a plan to put the late King Edward IV's brother, Richard Duke of Gloucester, on the throne. To do this it was necessary to intercept the party taking the twelve year old King Edward V to London for his coronation - due to take place a few days later. The two Dukes, Buckingham and Gloucester, rode to Stony Stratford, where the King was staying en route for London, dismissed his guards and took charge of the tearful, frightened boy. Richard then announced that his late brother's marriage had been invalid and declared young Edward a bastard and himself the rightful heir to the throne.

Richard was crowned in July 1483 and the renegade Duke of Buckingham saw his finest hour. With his huge retinue bearing the Stafford Knot livery, he was the acknowledged head of what was known as the 'old nobility' - although, of course, four hundred years before, the de Toeni-cum-Staffords had been very much a part of William the Conqueror's 'new nobility'.

The King heaped influential appointments and lucrative estates on to his ally Buckingham, in grateful thanks for the help he had received in misappropriating the crown. However, the Duke's part in obtaining possession of the traumatised young King Edward V, who then, along with his younger brother disappeared into the Tower never to be seen again, is surely one of the most horrible blots in the Stafford family's history.

Within months of implicating himself in this shabby child murder on King Richard's account, Buckingham changed sides yet again and raised an army in support of the Lancastrian claimant to the throne, Henry Tudor. It is possible that Buckingham had an ulterior motive - to take the throne himself - after all, he and Henry Tudor shared the same great-great-great grandfather in Edward III.

But this about-face was the high-flying Buckingham's downfall. His army deserted him and he was forced to flee and hide in the house of a servant who betrayed him for £1,000. On November 1st 1483 he was taken to Salisbury, where the following day he was executed and all his vast acquisitions became forfeit to the crown.

But this was not the end of the Staffords. When, two years later, Henry Tudor successfully seized the crown, he showed his recognition of the late Buckingham's efforts on his behalf by reinstating the dukedom on his seven year old son Edward. Edward's mother now married Jasper Tudor, the new King's uncle; the Staffords were yet again well connected in Court circles.

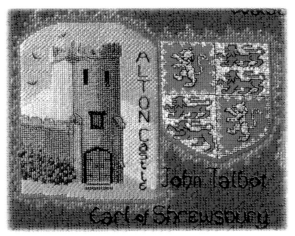

Yet another fortune-seeking Norman castle-builder was Bertrun de Verdun, who seems to have arrived in England at the behest of King Henry I early in the twelfth century. It was this family who in 1176 founded Croxden Abbey depicted in the thirteenth century panel (as an important part of Staffordshire's sheep farming industry, and possibly the sanctuary of King John's heart).

The de Verduns though were not destined to enjoy a lasting dynasty here in England, for after building his castle and founding his monastery, Bertrun went off to the Crusades with Richard the Lionheart and died in the Holy Land.

His heir was a grand-daughter whose son adopted the name Verdun and inherited Alton. But male heirs eluded this family and a century later, in 1316, the castle, which according to some near contemporary accounts was already a ruin, passed in marriage to the Fernivals of Sheffield who were well set up with estates of their own and didn't much care for their new Staffordshire appendage. Early in the century the Fernival heiress had married a Marcher Lord from the Welsh borders, John Talbot. John was a warrior who brought back from France tales of a young woman in white armour named Joan who had repulsed him from Orleans. For his services in France the Lancastrian King, Henry VI, created him Earl of Shrewsbury.

It was probably this man who rebuilt the crumbling Alton Castle, but we can leave the Talbot's for now as they crop up again in the next century.

The Wolseleys are another family like the Bagots and the Okeovers with an ancient Saxon pedigree, though no doubt, to keep their position in society, a fair amount of Norman blood had to be infused during medieval times.

There are deeds dating back to the time of William Rufus which make reference to the Wolseleys owning their land in the time of Edward the Confessor.

The name and the family arms of a wolf-dog seem to have been derived from wolves and leys and would suggest that the area where their cattle grazed (the leys) was frequently at risk from wolves roaming out of the near-by Cannock woods.

Although Staffordshire was mostly a Lancastrian stronghold, the Wolseleys were Yorkists and Ralph Wolseley was a great favourite with Edward IV who granted him many privileges including permission to enclose a park at Wolseley and stock it with deer from the forest.

Wolseley Hall may have been altered, remodelled and rebuilt many times, but it remained in the same place for possibly a thousand years, so generation upon generation of Wolseleys were reared in the same spot. Sadly, though, the family found themselves finally unable to maintain their ancestral hall and it was demolished early in the twentieth century.

Whether they were overly brave or incredibly inept, the chroniclers do not tell us, but the Staffordshire nobility certainly did their bit during the Wars of the Roses, when the Lancastrians and the Yorkists fought over the throne and spread their corpses liberally over the fields of England.

Except for the major blip of 1483, the Staffords were Lancastrian supporters and Edmund, the fifth Earl of Stafford, died for the cause at the Battle of Shrewsbury, 1403. The family suffered more loss when Humphrey, the 1st Duke of Buckingham, was slain at the Battle of Northampton in 1460. Humphrey's son had already been killed in 1455 at the Battle of St Albans.

The beheading in 1483 of the turn-coat Henry, the 2nd Duke of Buckingham, was also related to the Wars of the Roses.

The Audley family had intermarried with the Staffords and supported the House of Lancaster. Lord Audley lost his life along with 2000 of his men at the Battle of Blore Heath in 1459. Folklore tells us that Henry VI's Queen, Margaret, watched from the tower of Mucklestone church as the Lancastrians were routed in this blood bath, the only major battle of the Roses to be fought locally. Lord Dudley was also there, fighting for the Queen, and although he managed to dodge the arrows he was captured by the Yorkists.

The Battle of Northampton in 1460, where the 1st Duke of Buckingham fell, also claimed the life of another Staffordshire nobleman, John Talbot, the 2nd Earl of Shrewsbury who was fighting for the Yorkist cause.

Walter Devereux married the heiress of William, Lord Ferrers, in 1460 and so found himself the owner of a moated, timber mansion, Chartley Hall, as well as a long neglected and crumbling Chartley Castle. He also acquired a title, Baron Ferrers, to go with his ruin, and enjoyed his prominent position in society for twenty five years before dying alongside Richard III at the Battle of Bosworth.

During the Wars of the Roses the inn signs often displayed their loyalties to the Lord of the Manor on whose land they stood. Lions, both white and red, were linked to the Yorkist cause, whilst the swan was the badge of Henry Bolingbroke, the Duke of Lancaster, who became King Henry IV. Having said that, it has to be borne in mind that these nobles were not above swapping sides - the spectacular defection of the 2nd Duke of Buckingham to Richard III and then to Henry Tudor is just one example of how unreliable a guide to the lord's persuasions these signs might be.

The Earl of Stafford was not the only head of a Staffordshire family to die at the battle of Shrewsbury in 1403. The coats of arms of the knights, Sir William Handsacre and Sir Robert Mauveisyn represent a story of two families who supported opposing sides during the reign of the first Lancastrian King, Henry IV. Just three years previously Henry had taken the throne from Richard II and started the squabble that was to bloom into 'the Wars of the Roses'.

Sir Robert Mauveisyn, whose castle (long gone) was at Mauveisyn Ridware, received a call to arms and set out at the head of his band of make-shift soldiers to meet up with King Henry's forces at Shrewsbury. At the same time, his neighbour, a Yorkist, Sir William Handsacre, set forth at the head of his band of retainers to link up with Henry Percy 'Hotspur', who was plotting the new king's overthrow. The two contingents met, still within sight of home ground, and staged their own free-for-all. Sir William was killed by Sir Robert, who then carried on to Shrewsbury, where he too met his end. But the story doesn't finish there! After this double slaying, Sir Robert's daughter, Joanna, married Sir William Handsacre's son. Hardly the basis for a tranquil marriage - but the union probably had more to do with politics then any affinity between the two young people concerned.

In 1129, when Roger de Clinton was made Bishop of Lichfield, he found the ancient Saxon 'city' to be far short of his requirements and so he rebuilt the cathedral, fortified the close and laid out a new town with defensive ramparts and four access gates (known as barrs), patrolled by soldiers.

By this time St Chad's fame had travelled far and wide and the pilgrims, who flocked to pay their homage, found that arriving after curfew they were unable to get into the city as the gates were closed. To remedy this situation, the Bishop built a priory outside the Culstubbe Gate where the London road entered his city, and here travellers could obtain shelter and sustenance until the next morning. This was the origination of the Hospital of St John Baptist without the Barrs of the City of Lichfield.

By the time William Smith was consecrated Bishop of Lichfield in 1492, the ramparts and gates had long since fallen into disuse and travellers could wander freely into the city to find accommodation at will, leaving the priory as something of a lost cause. The Bishop therefore, found another use for St John's; he established a free grammar school there (the first evidence of a school in Lichfield), and also gave homes to 'thirteen honest, poor men upon whom the inconveniences of old age and poverty, without any fault of their own, have fallen'.

Sylvia chose to include St John's Hospital on this panel because of the extensive rebuilding work carried out by William Smith during this century. To accommodate the thirteen almsmen a new hall was built of red brick - one of the earliest examples of this material in Lichfield, and the eight tall, distinctive chimneys fronting St John Street provided each apartment with the comfort of its own hearth.

By the Middle Ages commerce was well established in Staffordshire along with a network of roads - perhaps rutted tracks is a better description - that gave merchants access to the markets and fairs where their goods could be traded. The plot of land often in front of the church that in the twelfth century had hosted the weekly market, was, by the end of this century, a designated area where permanent shops and stalls featured as well, along with a town clock and often a market hall.

The wool trade was still providing important revenue to the religious houses, with wool from Croxden Abbey fetching excellent prices abroad. Entrepreneurs were growing rich by manufacturing and exporting woollen cloth and there were mills at Burton, Tutbury, Uttoxeter and Himley.

In Walsall though, it was the leather and metal-working industries that made men rich and by the end of the century, the town was accepted as the centre for the manufacture of bits, stirrups and spurs and horse harness.

As the leather and metal-working industries became synonymous with Walsall in the South of Staffordshire, so the pottery trade became recognised in the north of the County, where Burslem is known as the Mother of the Potteries. Burslem is also the Bursley of Arnold Bennett's 'Five Towns'. Here the Adams family had established themselves with their rude domestic pottery by the middle of the fifteenth century -the brothers Richard and William were fined for digging clay by the side of the road in 1448. Venerable as their reputation is, the Adams family were by no means the first potters in North Staffordshire as kilns used in the early 14th century have been discovered at Sneyd Green.

The Closing Motif

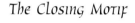

On 22nd August 1485, Henry Tudor's men hacked King Richard III to pieces at the Battle of Bosworth and Henry rewarded himself with the crown.

Fortunately for everyone concerned, King Edward IV had not got around to marrying off his elder daughter Elizabeth of York before he died, and it left the way clear for the new King Henry to marry the twenty year old Yorkist heir to the throne, and finally link the York and Lancaster dynasties and end the Wars of the Roses.

I suppose, as far as Elizabeth herself was concerned, she was just relieved that Henry Tudor was not already married, because with her strong claim to the throne, there was absolutely no way he would have allowed her to marry anyone else!

The first Tudors enjoyed a comparatively peaceful reign which allowed Henry to indulge his love of hunting in Needwood Forest and so Staffordshire was occasionally graced with the royal entourage. On such occasions they stayed at Tutbury Castle, which had become a royal estate when the Ferrers family fell from grace in the twelfth century.

The Fifteenth Century Embroidery Details

Purple is another background colour to avoid whenever possible - almost as harsh on my eyes as the red had been.

Without any doubt, the most difficult motif on this panel was John Talbot's shield. To get the tiny lions to look leonine in such a crowded space took quite a bit of ingenuity.

The roses of the opening and closing motifs were made from padded satin and couched round in gold and silver thread. The green leaves are made from silk, and the foliage is crafted in satin stitch.

The Stafford Knot is crafted entirely in tent stitch and couched round in gold braid.

The Sixteenth Century Embroidery Details

I struggled for hours over the onion-shaped domes of Tixall Gatehouse. These were worked on 12 count canvas directly onto the base canvas, and as they are only about one inch high, this means the curve of the onion was difficult to create without a stepped outline. I managed to achieve the effect seen here by over-stitching.

Baron Paget's ironworks was my first attempt at 'industrial embroidery', although I knew that with Staffordshire's later history, I was going to have to capture many more technological achievements with my needle and thread. This was one of the most intricate designs of the panels, and it included a tremendous amount of minute detail.

At this time, I still had not found leather needles to ease the task of embroidering the allegorical wind and little Spanish galleon of the closing motif.

The Sixteenth Century

Kings and Queens of the century

Henry VIII reigned 1509-1547. The first King of England to bear the title Majesty.

Edward VI reigned 1547-1553. This was Jane Seymour's child and she died within days of his birth. In spite of Henry's six wives, Edward was his only legitimate son.

Mary (Bloody Mary) 1553-1558. Married King Philip II of Spain. Mary was Henry's oldest child, born to Catherine of Aragon, his first Queen.

Elizabeth I (the Virgin Queen) reigned 1558-1603. Henry's second child, the daughter of Anne Boleyn.

The borders

Henry VIII is remembered more for his excess of wives, and particularly the manner in which he disposed of some of them, than for anything else that happened during his reign. He married Catherine of Aragon, Anne Boleyn, Jane Seymour, Anne of Cleves, Katherine Howard and Katherine Parr. There's a little rhyme to help you remember what happened to all of them:-

Divorced, beheaded, died
Divorced, beheaded, survived.

The Panel

The Opening Motif

This century was dominated by the schism in the church brought about, in part, because King Henry wanted to divorce Queen Catherine and marry Anne Boleyn, an action which the Pope would not sanction. Although Anne Boleyn seems popularly to attract the blame for the split with Rome, she was more a catalyst than the underlying reason, as Henry had long resented the power and authority that the Pope wielded over his realm.

Besides, as we have already seen, the Church had become incredibly wealthy and powerful during the past four hundred and fifty years since the Conquest. The ecclesiastics had become such proficient farmers and businessmen that, between them, the religious organisations now owned something like a third of all the land in England - more than the King himself, or any single noble.

With the separation of the English Church from Rome came the dissolution of the monasteries and the diminishing of the ecclesiastical power base in the country. An added benefit to Henry was the fact that he was able to plunder the incredible wealth of the religious houses - a welcome windfall to a profligate King.

The pious procession of monks, who had gone joyfully to their founding crosses during the eleventh and twelfth century panels, are now shown heads bowed, as their foundations were gradually suppressed.

The Benedictine priories of Canwell near Tamworth and of Sandwell in West Bromwich were amongst the first to go in 1525. The monks were transferred to other monasteries and the endowments which had supported them were used to establish a college at Oxford, Christ Church.

Once King Henry had the bit firmly between his teeth, this destructive anti-religious wave continued throughout his reign and was no doubt encouraged by his nobles and other landowners who were eagerly mopping up handsome properties and rich agricultural estates at knock-down prices. Burton Abbey, the oldest monastery in Staffordshire, held out until 1539.

The poor had been used to looking to the monks for charity before the dissolution. Now they found their new landlords and employers less charitably inclined and life became harsher for those who were unfortunate enough to fall out of work or become ill.

New money and a new gentry were very much in evidence this century as people from humble beginnings grasped the opportunities new and burgeoning industries provided. William Paget was a typical example. He started off, so tradition tells us, as the son of a Wednesbury nailer, and rose in Henry VIII's reign to become Lord Chancellor. It was Paget's task, as Chancellor, on 28th January 1547, to announce to the Houses of Parliament that the much married King was dead.

Earlier in Henry's Reformation reign, William had been there with his hand outstretched waiting for a share of the booty from the defunct monasteries, and he was granted not only the lands of the former Burton Abbey but also some of the manors previously belonging to the Bishops of Lichfield, among them Cannock, Rugeley, Smethwick, Tipton and Beaudesert where he made his principal residence.

He developed coalmining and ironworking on Cannock Chase and built the Midland's first known blast furnace there. Sylvia has based her portrayal of Baron Paget's ironworks on a drawing produced recently by archaeological architects who have excavated at the site. Her only qualm about the drawing was the fact that it showed the furnace to have a thatched roof! What, with all those sparks flying about?

Unfortunately, the advance in industrial achievement was not gained without losses in other areas. The heat required for making iron was obtained by burning trees and Paget was granted a licence in 1560 to fell trees on the Chase for that purpose. By the end of this century Cannock Chase had been, more or less, stripped of timber which meant that the deer population declined dramatically. There was, in fact, a two pronged attack on the Chase, for the trees that weren't disappearing into Paget's ironworks, were being cleared to make way for his sheep farming activities. Between 1582 and the turn of the century he increased his head of sheep from 6,200 to 6,700. There is more about the fortunes (and misfortunes) of the Paget family in the 19th century panel.

Another 'local man made good' was Gilbert Sheldon who was born at Stanton in the north of the County in 1598. From humble beginnings Gilbert rose to become Bishop of London and Archbishop of Canterbury, although later he fell out of favour with Charles II for denouncing the King's gross immorality and refusing him Holy Communion. He amassed great wealth - sufficient to be able to instruct Christopher Wren to build the Sheldonian Theatre at Oxford.

In Barton-under-Needwood there was another family who fared well during this century. In their simple cottage, the Taylor family were blessed with a set of healthy, male triplets, an event so very rare that when King Henry VII came on one of his hunting expeditions to Needwood Forest, the children were presented to him, and he ordered that they were to be cared for. Presumably the royal instructions were backed with funds, for all three boys thrived and received a good education - so much so that one of them, John, rose to the eminence of secretary to King Henry VIII. To this John Taylor, the people of Barton owe their church - and the name of their school.

John Holland of Newcastle-under-Lyme was one of only two frying pan manufacturers in sixteenth century England. Perhaps Sylvia wanted to remind us of the famous Staffordshire oatcakes with this picture - or perhaps it was because of the inordinate number of quick bacon butties rustled up in her frying pan during the five and a half years that these embroideries were in the making!

Although schooling was available as far back as the late 1300s, little is known about the methods of teaching or the social standing of the people who were in charge of the scholars. We know that in 1380 a Stafford schoolteacher by the name of Thomas was one of a group pardoned for aiding and abetting a murder, and that in 1397 John Pepard, who had been teaching the son of a Richard Bowers, was forced to sue for tuition fees. Whether Bowers was unable to meet his commitments or Pepard was an inept teacher, undeserving of payment, the chronicles don't tell us.

Wolverhampton's Free Grammar School was founded by Sir Stephen Jenyns, a native of the town, who became a London merchant-tailor, in 1512. There was just one master at the school and there was no pre-requisite to live in the town to gain admittance, but it was necessary to be literate in English and to know the catechism in English and Latin. The curriculum looks incredibly boring and narrow today, the boys learning from Terence, Ovid, Horace, Virgil, Cicero, Isocrates, Zenophon and Homer.

Thomas Alleyne bequeathed property in several counties to Trinity College,

Cambridge, with instructions that they were to endow free grammar schools at various places including Stone and Uttoxeter. Alleyne stipulated that children living within two or three miles of the schools (who were required to have a firm knowledge of grammar) were to be educated free of charge and that the masters could supplement their incomes by taking in fee paying children from further afield. The masters (one at each school) were paid an annual salary of £13. 6s. 8d. for which they taught from 6am to 11am and 1pm to 5 pm with one free afternoon weekly, seven days holiday at Whitsun and ten days at Easter. Alleyne's instructions also insisted that the pupils were to talk to each other in Latin at all times, in and out of school hours.

Walsall Grammar School owes its existence to an Act of Parliament passed in 1547 during the reign of King Edward VI. All endowments of convents, chapels and chantries not so far repressed became the property of the Crown and the revenue obtained was for the building of almshouses, grammar schools and hospitals - although this was often not where the money was channelled. The tithes of the rectory of Walsall somehow slipped into the pocket of John Dudley, owner of Dudley Castle, Lord of the Manor of Walsall and one of the King's chief advisers. When Dudley was executed (in the year Queen Mary came to the throne) and his estates forfeited to the Crown, the people of Walsall, headed by Nicholas and George Hawe, mounted a petition asking Mary to allow the money 'misappropriated' by Dudley to be, henceforth, directed towards the founding of a Grammar School.

The school still maintains an annual Founder's Day tradition commemorating the grant of the subsequent charter in 1554. On the first Friday in July the headmaster, the school captain, the first year boys and their masters, and some old scholars, make the journey to Westminster Abbey where the outgoing school captain and the youngest boy together lay a wreath on Queen Mary's tomb.

During the six years reign of young Edward VI, the Country had on the whole learned to accept quite peaceably the changes to their religion. A new prayer book written in English instead of Latin was adopted in 1552 and a more Protestant doctrine was established.

But then the sixteen year old King died and his Catholic half-sister Mary ascended the throne. Mary was determined to restore England to full obedience to the Pope and to cleanse the land of heresy. The persecutions of King Henry VIII's reign started all over again, but this time it was the Protestants who suffered.

Plaques along the walls of St Mary's Church tell of the execution of heretics in the market square just outside the church doors. Thomas Hayward and John Goreway were burned at the stake in September 1555. The Sheriff of Lichfield was reluctant to despatch a third heretic, Joyce Lewis, the wife of a farmer

from nearby Mancetter. Joyce had embraced Protestantism, and she turned her back on the altar during a service which her Catholic husband had insisted she attend. On 18th December 1557 a new Sheriff with less scruples had the sentence carried out. Joyce supposedly smiled serenely throughout her ordeal.

The market square outside the church where the atrocities took place is still cobbled as it was four hundred and fifty years ago. Another interesting plaque tells us that one Edward Wightman, a heretic of Burton-on-Trent perished at the stake there on 11th April 1612. It states that this unfortunate fellow was the last person in England so to die. (But, for the record, as Bloody Mary died in 1558, this one is not down to her).

Another family to further their fortunes this century were the Levesons of Wolverhampton. They had made their money in the wool trade in the fourteenth century and then married into the gentry - social mobility at its most effective. As with the Pagets, the Levesons were happy to avail themselves of bargain property deals in the middle of the century as the religious estates came on to the market. The family acquired Trentham Priory near Newcastle-under-Lyme,where they built a grand hall in the 1630s, and where later generations would entertain royalty in lavish style.

Vice-Admiral Sir Richard Leveson, whose bronze statue stands in St Peter's Church, Wolverhampton, is probably the most colourful of the Levesons. In 1588 he was an eighteen year old volunteer on the Ark Royal and fought under Drake against the Armada. He rose swiftly through Queen Elizabeth's navy to command a fleet of ships hunting down the Spanish treasure galleons. His days of legalised piracy were spectacularly successful and in recognition of the booty he brought home he was made an admiral for life, but he died at the early age of thirty five before he had long to enjoy his title.

During this century, the towns and villages with raw materials to exploit began to industrialise, outstripping other communities. Burslem for instance, where a hundred years before the Adams Family had established their business from the clay about their feet, now progressed from strength to strength. Villages like Brewood, on the other hand, without any natural resources ceased to keep pace. It remains to this day a village with 'olde worlde' charm and a parish council determined to keep it so.

In the south of the County, where all but Wolverhampton, Walsall and Dudley (which does not really count as only the castle belonged to Staffordshire) was woodland, heath and a few small scattered villages, they gradually discovered how to utilise their iron and coal deposits. Each area developed its own speciality -Willenhall made locks, Walsall made horse 'furniture', both metal and leather, and Sedgley became synonymous with nail making.

'Nailing' embraced nuts, bolts, screws, sprigs, tacks and clouts and was considered to be less skilful than other trades such as scythemaking or lockmaking and so paid less. The nails were made in small, dark workshops at the back of the nailer's home and, to make sufficient money to exist, it was necessary for the wife and children to work long, gruelling hours alongside him.

Littletons can be traced back to the reign of Henry II but they were not connected with Staffordshire at that time. These Littletons were courtiers and one, Thomas de Littleton was Squire of the Body of Henry IV and V - an extremely trustworthy position. Thomas married the heiress of Richard Quatremains and their only child married Thomas Westcote a courtier in the service of Henry VI.

To preserve the Littleton name, the Westcotes' adopted their mother's illustrious surname and it was the eldest of these Westcote-cum-Littletons whose youngest son Richard married the Pillaton heiress and brought the Littletons into Staffordshire.

Having arrived here, up until the time of the Civil War they seem to have kept a remarkably low profile. Even the fact that they were Catholic during the years when adherence to the Pope could be a life threatening option does not seem to have brought any notable drama into their lives, as it did the Giffards. The senior branch of the family found themselves on the wrong side of the impoverished owner of Dudley Castle in 1592. Edward Lord Dudley, with 140 men armed with arrows, bill hooks and staves, raided two of the Littleton properties in the middle of the night and drove away over 300 sheep, some oxen and a bull. Several of the raided cattle were slaughtered and eaten by the time the bailiff turned up at the Castle four days later to investigate Littleton's complaint. Lord Dudley's servants threatened to cut the officer and his men to pieces and chased them away. Goodness knows what the Littletons had done to upset the Dudleys - history does not tell us.

Mary Queen of Scots fled Scotland in May 1568 and took refuge in England, where she expected Protestant Queen Elizabeth to greet her as a distant cousin and fellow Queen. Instead Elizabeth imprisoned her Catholic relative as a threat to the English throne. At first Mary was kept at Bolton Castle in Wensleydale, but there were so many intrigues surrounding her that she was brought further south to Staffordshire and Tutbury Castle. Castles were no longer 'desirable residences'. Tutbury was being used as a hunting lodge by its owner, George Talbot, the 6th Earl of Shrewsbury. George has always been more famous for being the long suffering fourth husband of Bess of Hardwick, than for being gaoler to Mary Queen of Scots, which was a thankless task, a continual worry and a financial burden to him. Mary was allowed a retinue of fifty staff including two live-in physicians and Talbot was allocated an utterly insufficient £52 per week for her maintenance. Queen Elizabeth turned a deaf ear to his fiscal problems - which, in truth, were not acute - he and his wife owned several huge estates.

Mary was moved after a short while to another of Talbot's manors, Wingfield in Derbyshire. Life was far more comfortable there, but it was not long before a plot was uncovered which involved assassinating Queen Elizabeth, marrying Mary to the Duke of Norfolk, and placing them on the throne. Norfolk was executed and Mary was hauled back to Tutbury with a reduction in her staff and much tighter supervision.

Another conspiracy to rescue the Scot's Queen was hatched up by the northern earls who decided to storm Tutbury. It was an ill-managed plot which in its failure brought acclaim to Walter Devereux - whose ancestor had married the Ferrers heiress a hundred years before and obtained the Chartley estates. The Devereux family had been making their way quite successfully since this useful matrimonial alliance, and when Walter raised troops to suppress the northern earls' rebellion his grateful Queen created him Earl of Essex for his trouble.

Now Mary's plight was worse than ever; the lock of her outer chamber door was removed and she had no privacy to receive visitors. A letter she wrote describes just how miserable the Tutbury lodgings were: *I am in a walled enclosure on the top of a hill, exposed to all the winds and inclemencies of heaven. Within the enclosure there is a very old hunting lodge, built of timber and plaster cracked in all parts........*

She describes it as being situated so low that the earth ramparts behind the wall were on a level with the roof of the building obscuring the sunshine and light. There was a foul stench from the Castle's privies which were near to her rooms. All right for the 'lads' on a week's hunting trip, but not quite the place to incarcerate a twenty eight year old Queen!

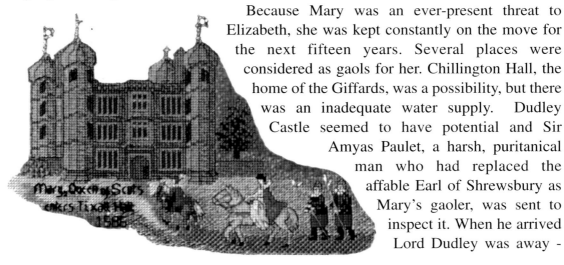

Because Mary was an ever-present threat to Elizabeth, she was kept constantly on the move for the next fifteen years. Several places were considered as gaols for her. Chillington Hall, the home of the Giffards, was a possibility, but there was an inadequate water supply. Dudley Castle seemed to have potential and Sir Amyas Paulet, a harsh, puritanical man who had replaced the affable Earl of Shrewsbury as Mary's gaoler, was sent to inspect it. When he arrived Lord Dudley was away -

which may have been because he did not want, and could not afford, to host Mary. Sir Amos eventually gained access to the castle and in his report to Sir Francis Walsingham he wrote "....finding my Lord Dudley absent I was forced to take my lodging in one of the poorest towns I have seen in my life." Was this Dudley's first bad press? It seems that amongst other problems the Castle's brewing vessels were in a state of decay, and so, in 1585, Mary was taken to Chartley Manor, owned by the 2nd Earl of Essex, Robert Devereux, a young man who was not even consulted by Queen Elizabeth and her ministers before he was made the royal guest's landlord.

It was here that the Giffards became involved in the Babbington Plot which sealed Mary's unhappy fate. Gilbert Giffard agreed to act as a double agent for Walsingham who was paranoid in his fear that the Scot's Queen - now debilitated with rheumatism - was still capable of whipping up Catholic sympathisers to assassinate Elizabeth and place Mary on the throne. Coded messages to Mary, outlining just such a plan, were given by Giffard to a Burton brewer, who concealed them in his beer barrels and delivered them to Chartley Manor. Replies were smuggled out in the same way and passed to Giffard - and thence to Walsingham.

The central panel shows Mary arriving at the gatehouse to Tixall Hall where she had been brought on the promise of a day's hunting. Instead she was met by a party of horsemen with a warrant to detain her at the Hall while her rooms at Chartley were searched. Letters found there evidenced a plot to overthrow Queen Elizabeth.

Mary Queen of Scots' execution in February 1587 meant one less threat to Elizabeth's throne, but her brother-in-law, King Philip of Spain, was still intent on seizing the English throne and returning the English to the Catholic faith.

Philip launched his Armada of 130 grand galleons against Elizabeth's navy of 38 vessels and a flotilla of willing sea-dogs. After almost a week of scrapping in the Channel, the Spanish anchored off Calais to wait for reinforcements from the Netherlands. In the night the English sent fire-ships across to them and the Spanish, in a hopeless panic, cut their cables and sailed out to sea. Amongst squalls and blinding rain, the English were waiting to fire on them. With their superior seamanship and lighter, more manoeuvrable craft, the English outclassed their foes, until the wind changed, giving the Spanish the chance to make for the North Sea. The Armada had no choice but to sail up the east coast of England around the British Isles. With insufficient food, rancid water and Drake chasing them as far as the Firth of Forth, less than 70 of the galleons reached Santander.

Sylvia closes the panel with a fulsome silver wind blasting the Spanish Armada and the words from Elizabeth I's Armada medal.

The Closing Motif

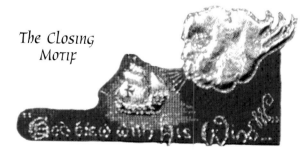

The Seventeenth Century

Charles I   Charles II

1600   James I   Commonwealth

The Compleat Angler

The Siege of Lichfield Close 1646

Isaac Walton b. Stafford 1653

Wrottesley

Glassworks at Bagot's Wood

County Sheriff

E. Ras Ashmole b. Lichfield 1617

Siege of Holbeche House Kingswinford Gunpowder Plot 1605

Death Warrant Charles I
John Bradshaw MP for Stafford
Thos. Harrison Mayor of Newcastle

Willenhall

Silk Spinners of Leek

Newcastle   Salt   Shirleywich

Jane Lane of Bentley Hall aids Charles II escape after the Battle of Worcester 1651

W + M

James II   William III + Mary II   1700

Lichfield District Council

Rolleston-on-Dove

Kings and Queens of the century

James I (the wisest fool in Christendom) reigned 1603-1625. First Stuart king and the only child of Mary Queen of Scots. Married Anne, daughter of the King of Denmark.

Charles I reigned 1625-1649. Married Henrietta Maria, sister of the King of France. Although several kings of England met untimely deaths, his execution was the only time that the reigning monarch was officially 'done to death' - although, we managed a practise run on his grandmother, Mary Queen of Scots, 62 years before.

The Commonwealth 1649-1660. Oliver Cromwell.

Charles II (The Merry Monarch) reigned 1660-1685. Married Catherine of Braganza, daughter of the King of Portugal. Although he had no legitimate heirs, he sired a prodigious amount of offspring - with descendants amongst today's aristocracy.

James II reigned 1685-1689. Charles II's brother. Married Anne Hyde and then Mary of Modena.

William III and Mary II reigned 1689-1694 (Mary) -1702 (William). Mary was James II's daughter by Anne Hyde. William, Prince of Orange, was Mary's husband.

The borders

In 1649, when Charles I was executed, the Monarchy, the House of Lords and the Anglican Church were abolished and England became a republic.

Oliver Cromwell was a gentleman sheep farmer from Huntingdon who rose to great prominence during the quarrels between Charles I and Parliament. He was instrumental in the King's execution and afterwards, during the Commonwealth, he became chairman of the Council of State. In 1653 he dissolved Parliament and took over as Lord Protector. For five years Cromwell was virtually a dictator and when he died his son Richard took command. But the younger Cromwell was not strong enough to hold the Republic together and in 1660 Charles II was invited to return as King.

R olleston-on-Dove is here representative of the rich pastures of the Dove and Trent valleys which enabled farmers to supply the growing London market with butter and cheese. As early as 1540 it was reported that 'there be wonderful pastures upon the Dove', and a hundred years later these meadows were being exploited so successfully that the London cheesemongers had set up an agency in Uttoxeter to handle the trade. Dairy

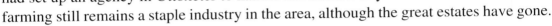

farming still remains a staple industry in the area, although the great estates have gone.

W hen Whitwick Ladies Coffee Club first saw the panels, a butterfly shared this space with James II, but Sylvia felt she could not refuse their special request, and so it had to be unpicked. The coffee pot which replaced the butterfly represents all of the small clubs throughout the County who work quietly to raise funds for various charities - Whitwick Ladies just wanted the people of Staffordshire to be reminded they are out there.

The Panel

Sylvia's opening motif, the silver Scottish unicorn clasping the Scottish Arms between its hoofs, indicates the accession of the first Stuart monarch to the throne of England when James VI of Scotland reigned as James I. James was the only child of Mary Queen of Scots and her husband Lord Darnley, murdered when his son was less than a year old. That same year, 1567, Mary was forced to abdicate her throne and flee to England and eventual execution. James never knew his parents.

The Openinç Motif

Although the Virgin Queen, Elizabeth I, had steadfastly refused to name a successor throughout her 44 year reign, the story survives that on her death bed she indicated that Mary's son should succeed her. Whether Elizabeth did actually give her nearest kinsman her blessing we will never know, but the vast majority of her subjects were happy enough for a Protestant, descended directly from the first Tudor monarch, to be their King.

No sooner was James I on the English throne in 1603 than there was a plot to remove him. James had made a promise to be more lenient with the Recusants (Catholics who refused to attend the Church of England services). This did not last long and soon the Catholics were facing even heavier fines than in Elizabeth's reign.

A conspiracy was hatched to place a Roman Catholic sovereign on the throne. The first phase was to blow up the Houses of Parliament during the opening ceremony, when the King, his two sons and his ministers would be there. It all went badly wrong, and on the night of 4th November 1605 Guy Fawkes was discovered in a cellar underneath the House of Lords with a cache of gunpowder. The other conspirators fled London and made their way to Stephen Littleton's home, Holbeach House, in Himley, getting their gunpowder supply wet as they crossed the River Stour.

While they were holed up there awaiting the Sheriff and his men, an accident happened which, all things considered, was probably apt punishment for those who had been prepared to annihilate so many innocent victims along with their target. A dish holding some of the damp gunpowder was drying near the fire when a live ember toppled into it and caused a huge explosion severely burning two of the conspirators, including the ringleader Robert Catesby and blinding a third, Francis Grant. Curiously, the explosion carried a bag of gunpowder through the roof  without igniting it, so instead of a loud bang and instant oblivion, the fate of those who survived the Sheriff's shoot-out was a journey to the Tower of London, and a traitor's death, which meant being hung, drawn and quartered.

Two of the desperadoes, Stephen Littleton and Robert Winter escaped into the woods and lived rough around the Rowley area for several days, relying on farmers sympathetic to their plight. Eventually they made their way to Hagley House where Stephen's brother Humphrey Littleton lived. Humphrey's cook fed the starving men and then went to the village on the excuse of fetching liquor, and shopped them. For this service the cook was granted a life pension from state funds.

Londoners were not the only ones to enjoy the executions, although of course, they did get to have the star of the show, Guy Fawkes, who had been tortured to such an extent that he was hardly able to climb the steps to the scaffold. Humphrey Littleton and a few other plotters were despatched at Worcester, and Staffordshire dealt with Stephen Littleton and the Rowley farmers who had sustained him on the run. As a gruesome finale, the Sheriff of Staffordshire was instructed to exhume Robert Catesby and Thomas Percy and have them quartered and displayed.

When Civil War broke out in August 1642, the common folk of Staffordshire were, on the whole, quite indifferent to King Charles I's problems and would have preferred not to get involved. When they were at last dragged into the fighting, they had little choice but to follow their Lord's persuasion, so the recruits to Lord Paget's regiment were Parliamentarians (Roundheads) as long as Paget supported Parliament, and became Royalist when he swapped sides.

The King's headquarters were at Oxford, but the ports loyal to his cause were to the north, so it was important to hold the Midlands, especially Lichfield with the main road to Oxford passing through it. For this reason, Staffordshire saw more than its share of action as the armies of both sides crossed and re-crossed the County in attempts to either gain or keep control of strategic locations, such as the bridge over the Trent at Burton, and Tamworth, Stafford, Tutbury, Dudley, and of course, Lichfield.

Almost as soon as the war began the Cathedral City was garrisoned by Royalists who fortified the Close. The Parliamentarians soon appeared on the scene and rounding up some local womenfolk and children forced them into the Close, where, huddled together and frightened for their lives, they were forced to endure the cross-fire of the siege. The Royalists soon surrendered under this psychological warfare and the Roundheads took control of the Cathedral where they wreaked havoc, destroying monuments, defacing sculptures and even stabling their horses inside the building.

Within two months the Royalists regained the Cathedral area. They brought in miners from south Staffordshire who tunnelled under the wall of the Close, packed the cavity with explosives and then blew it up, thus demolishing part of the wall. A Royalist garrison was left in the town and Richard Bagot was appointed Governor. Richard was to die a few years later in 1646 when the Royalists were savagely beaten at the Battle of Naseby in Northamptonshire.

In the year that Charles I ascended his throne, the owner of Stafford Castle, young Edward Stafford, died. He had married Isobel Forster from Tong who was one of his grandmother's maids and at his death Isobel was left with huge debts and a young son and daughter to rear. The son died aged sixteen . His sister, the heiress, married one of the Earl of Arundel's younger sons and so, at the time of the Civil War, Stafford Castle passed into the Howard family. The newly married couple went off to live in London and left the dowager Isobel at the Castle which she stoutly defended for several weeks before submitting to Sir William Brereton's Roundhead forces.

Tutbury Castle was well stocked with supplies and did not surrender until April 1646 when the plague broke out amongst the garrisoned Royalist troops.

Meanwhile Dudley Castle, which the impecunious 9th Lord Dudley had recently traded to a London goldsmith named Humble Ward along with his estates and his grand-daughter, was under the Royalist commander Colonel Leveson. There was an attempt by the Roundheads to lay siege to the Castle although the fighting eventually took place away towards Tipton. After a three hour battle, with considerable casualties but no conclusive result, the Roundheads withdrew and the Castle remained in Royalists hands until Leveson surrendered it, without bloodshed in May 1646.

And so it was that by July of 1646 Lichfield alone in Staffordshire still held out against the Parliamentarians. After Richard Bagot's death at Naseby, his younger brother Hervy took over as Governor until a more senior officer was appointed. It was Hervy and the new Governor whose refusal to surrender caused the Roundheads under Colonel Brereton to spend five days bombarding the highest steeple of the Cathedral so that it eventually toppled, bringing surrender in its wake.

A Staffordshire man, John Bradshaw, presided over the court at King Charles' trial and gave out the death sentence. The King tried to speak but Bradshaw declared that a prisoner was never heard once sentence had been pronounced and Charles was hustled away. Bradshaw's name heads the list of fifty-nine people who signed the death warrant (Oliver Cromwell's name is third) and although the risk of assassination at the time of the trial was such that he had a metal-reinforced hat made, he lived to prosper and 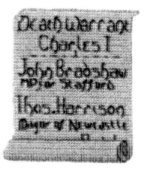 become M.P. for Stafford and Cheshire. Another Staffordshire regicide who sat at the King's trial and signed the death warrant was Thomas Harrison, four times mayor of Newcastle-under-Lyme.

Bradshaw had exquisite timing - he died in 1659 - but Harrison was alive when Charles II regained the throne a year later, was brought to trial and put to death. The event was watched and recorded by the great diarist Samuel Pepys who wrote "I went to Charing Cross, to see Major-General Harrison hanged, drawn and quartered, which was done there, he looking as cheerful as any man could do in that condition."

Charles Stuart was living in France when his father Charles I was executed in 1649. Scotland was quite outraged at what had happened to their King - this was after all Mary Queen of Scots' great-grandson. The English looked to be making a habit of decapitating Scottish monarchs.

They invited the nineteen year old Charles to Scotland and proclaimed him King of England, Ireland and Scotland in 1650. A year later the King marched a Scots' army into England and down to the Midlands where, on Wednesday 3rd September, they engaged with Cromwell's soldiers at Worcester. By evening it was clear that the battle was lost and Charles with about sixty trusted allies, including Henry, Lord

Wilmot, slipped away under cover of darkness and rode into Staffordshire, entering the County at Kinver. Another of the party was Charles Giffard of Chillington Hall, near Brewood, who was now on home ground, and so, with his servant Francis Yates, led the way to White Ladies. This property was owned by Giffard and leased to the Penderel family. Here Charles and his companions separated, each to make their own escape from Cromwell's troops who were already scouring the area.

Richard Penderel took charge of Charles early the next morning. He hacked off the young King's hair, gave him a change of clothes and accompanied him into Boscobel Wood to spend the day hiding in the remote Spring Coppice. That night Penderel and Charles set out to walk the nine miles to Madeley where the intention was that the King would cross the River Severn and make his way into Wales. Shortly before they reached Madeley they were challenged by a miller and had to run and hide, not knowing whether the man was friend or foe. They eventually reached the house of an acquaintance of Penderel who warned them that the area was seething with Roundhead soldiers and that the Severn crossings were closely guarded. So, after spending the day hiding in a barn, Charles and Penderel returned across country and made their way to Boscobel House in the early hours of the morning.

Another Royalist refugee, Major Carless, was already in hiding at Boscobel House. The two of them left before day-break to seek shelter in the wood where they climbed into an oak tree. There they watched Cromwell's soldiers beating about in the thickets below them. Charles found this sojourn in the tree so uncomfortable that he decided he would rather risk staying that night, and the following day, in Boscobel House and grounds. Food had to be provided and Major Carless availed himself of a sheep from a neighbour's fold. The animal was hastily butchered and cooked, with Charles himself taking a hand with the frying pan. That evening all five Penderel brothers led Charles to Moseley Hall at Fordhouses, near Wolverhampton, where Lord Wilmot came to see him. Wilmot, after fleeing the Battle of Worcester, had found sanctuary with Colonel Lane and his sister Jane at Bentley Hall near Walsall. They

had hatched up an escape plan for Wilmot, which pivoted on Jane having obtained a pass for herself and a man-servant to visit a friend in Bristol. Wilmot was to travel as Jane's servant, but he gallantly offered his escape route to Charles.

Stories abound of the long, slow journey to Bristol when Jane rode pillion behind 'Will Jackson'. One tells how Jane caused the horse to splash some of Cromwell's soldiers and then berated and cuffed her 'manservant' for being so clumsy. Another anecdote claims that when the horse cast a shoe, 'Will Jackson' chatted with the blacksmith about the fate of Charles Stuart and agreed that if the rogue were caught, he should be hanged.

The families who helped Charles to get away from England seriously imperilled their own lives by so doing. There was a £1,000 price on his head and his description, a 'tall black man upwards of two yards high' was distributed all over the region. His exceptional height (inherited from his great-grandparents Mary Queen of Scots and Darnley who were both 'six footers') could have been an instant give-away to the enemy if they sighted him, and ruination, if not death, to anyone found in his company.

The Penderels were given a gruelling cross examination by the Roundheads shortly after Charles left Boscobel House, and the property, along with White Ladies was thoroughly searched. Although Charles Giffard escaped, his servant Francis Yates was executed for his part in leading the King from Kinver to White Ladies.

After the Restoration, Charles did not forget the Penderels or the Lanes. Pensions were granted to the brothers Penderel in perpetuity and are still paid to this day! To Colonel Lane the King offered burial at Westminster Abbey. This illustrious entombment was declined, the Colonel settling instead for a pension of £500 a year, a Royal canton on his coat of arms and a plaque in St Peters Church, Wolverhampton.

An interesting point here - Jane Lane's grandmother was Jane, the daughter of Sir Edward Littleton of Pillaton Hall. So, while half a century before, members of the Himley and Hagley branches of the Littleton family came to drastic ends trying to get rid of James I, now a member of the Pillaton branch was risking her neck to help James' grandson gain the throne.

B orn the son of an Elizabethan alehouse keeper, Izaac Walton of Stafford was a grown man before the County split into Royalists and Parliamentarians. As a young man Walton moved to London where he met and became friends with John Donne and many other great men. Although his livelihood was in the capital, Walton frequently returned to his native Staffordshire to indulge his love of angling with his friend Charles Cotton.

Sylvia's cameo shows him at his favourite pastime at Pike Pool, where a timeless limestone pillar rises free standing from clear, shallow waters. It was on one of these trips home that Walton was to become involved in something far less tranquil than fishing. In 1651, King Charles II, who was fighting to regain his birthright, was forced to flee for his life after the Battle of Worcester went badly against him. His possessions were divided amongst loyal followers and one large jewel, known as the Lesser George, was entrusted to a Colonel Blagg who, having hidden from the Roundheads at Broughton Hall, was forced to move on and leave the jewel with the Hall's owner, George Barlow. Barlow gave the jewel to Walton and later Colonel Blagg retrieved it from him in London and returned it to King Charles, by then in France. Trivial as it may seem, such an act would have put Walton at great personal risk. Two years after this episode, when Walton was sixty, he published his famous book, The Compleat Angler.

Elias Ashmole was born in Lichfield in 1617, and, after being educated at the local grammar school, he moved to London. Here he studied law until the Civil War broke out when he joined the King's forces. After the restoration he was introduced as a staunch supporter of the King's cause to Charles II, and for a short time he became a courtier.

Later, Ashmole lodged in London with an antiquarian named Tradescant who had assembled a valuable collection of curiosities which he eventually handed over to the younger man. Ashmole subsequently presented the collection to Oxford University along with many additions of his own. This was the beginnings of the oldest museum in Britain, the Ashmolean, founded in 1683.

In 1637 Staffordshire was described as being mostly barren land with about a quarter heath and waste and another quarter chases and parks. Many of the parks were well stocked with deer before the ravages of the Civil War, but later in the century deer-parks went out of favour and country-house parks became the fashion. Trees were uprooted, rivers diverted, lakes excavated and formal gardens created within the newly enclosed country-house parks, and if the local village happened to disfigure the view, then it had to go. Many villages disappeared at this time in the quest for a perfect vista from the Lord's hall.

The Wrottesleys, descended in direct male line from Simon de Wrottesley in 1164, took their name from the village where they settled - and then when it became fashionable to lay out a country-house park, they swept the villagers away because their huddle of houses spoilt the view across the newly designed landscape. Other villages that went the same way as Wrottesley include Blithfield and Chillington. The latter disappeared in the 1750s when the park was laid out by Capability Brown. The park is still there  today and the sheep still roam to within yards of the imposing, porticoed front door of the present John Giffard's 18th century hall.

During the hundred years 1560 to 1660, the County's population doubled from 10,000 to 20,000, and to support these extra people, common and waste land had to be brought under cultivation and subjected to new farming methods. This caused a great deal of hardship for the common folk who had always depended upon their inherited rights to use the common pasture lands now disappearing.

However, other methods of making a living were fast developing. Industry had arrived and was demanding a labour force to make use of the newly developing technologies. The ancestors of the feudal lords who had jumped on William the Conqueror's bandwagon 600 years ago, could no longer rely on the rent from their vast land holdings to keep them in the grand manner. They turned into businessmen competing with the Johnny-come-latelys like the Levesons and Pagets.

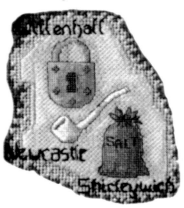

To denote the beginnings of this burgeoning commercial Staffordshire, Sylvia has depicted three of the industries which gathered momentum in the 1600s, as old skills were honed and new ones learned. Pottery continued to be produced, predominantly in the north of Staffordshire, with Burslem specialising in butter pots for the Dove valley's famous dairy produce, and Newcastle in clay pipes. Metalworking took over in the south of the County. Gunmaking developed in Wednesbury, Darlaston, Harborne (and Dudley), nail making of all shapes and sizes continued as the back-yard industry of Sedgley. Willenhall, the town where lock making won acclaim and the craftsman's labours curved his spine, became known as Humpshire.

The Devereux-cum-Ferrers family, now the Earls of Essex, started the century on a down beat, when Robert the 2nd Earl got on the wrong side of Queen Elizabeth and had his head cut off. His son, also Robert, found favour with James I and had the Earldom restored, and then, rather ungraciously, became Chief of the Parliamentary forces during the Civil War. This Earl died childless - a disastrous arranged marriage when he was fourteen ended in divorce - and his sister's grandson, Sir Robert Shirley, inherited the Chartley estates. Shirley was a man with an eye for business, and he developed brine springs to produce salt at Weston-on-Trent. By 1690 his enterprise was in full swing and the area became known as Shirleywich after the family name.

By the last quarter of the century, Leek had forged a profitable niche for itself in the silk industry. There is little proof to back the popular theory that Huguenot refugees from France passed the skills onto the townspeople. The first date connecting the textile business with Leek appears in the parish register when in 1636 Richard Malking is described as a texator. State protection by the prohibition of French manufactured silks gave a boost to the Leek spinners' at the end of the century and again in 1701 when Indian and Chinese silks were barred. Parliament again helped to protect the silk spinners livelihood when in 1720 an Act was passed prohibiting the wearing of buttons and button-holes made of cloth or serge.

We left the Bagots in charge of a herd of goats back in the 14th century, and have barely mentioned them since. It is not that they avoided involvment in the politics and wars of the County, it is rather that they did not take star parts. They did not aspire to great wealth, palaces or titles and so they never attained such importance that any ruler felt the need to cut off their heads. They mixed and married with the powerful families of Buckingham, Essex and Dudley (all to lose a few heads), but somehow, they managed to remain on the fringe of events when heads were toppling.

Tudor times were difficult for the landed gentry with inflation eating into their fixed rental incomes. Several ancient families sold out to successful business men and lawyers anxious to buy their way into the upper classes. The feckless gambling Edward, Lord Dudley, who sold out to Humble Ward, a London goldsmith, is a perfect example of this trade-to-aristocracy transition.

The Bagots took to industry to supplement their income. Early in the century, glaziers, who had arrived from Lorraine in Tudor times, were working in Bagot's Park where there was plenty of timber for the process.

And the goats? - they are no longer at Blithfield, but you can see them, along with the genetically modified Chartley Cattle, at the Cotswold Farm Park.

The Closing Motif

Charles II reigned for twenty-five years, but died without a legitimate heir. His brother James II, who was a Roman Catholic, ruled for the next four years. James caused so much religious friction that he was forced to send his wife and young son to France for safety and followed himself just before Christmas 1688. The House of Commons declared that he had, by fleeing, abdicated - although this had not been his intention. Nonetheless the following February, William of Orange - a grandson of Charles I, and his wife Mary, who was James' daughter by his first wife, were declared King and Queen. Sylvia's conjoined crowns acknowledge the fact that this was the only time during the millennium when England was ruled by a joint King and Queen each in their own right.

The Seventeenth Century Embroidery Details

I was halfway through attaching the unicorn in this panel when I discovered leather needles, and oh, what a relief for my poor fingers. These triangular needles are not the normal stock-in trade of an embroiderer's shop, but you should be able to find them in any decent craft shop.

Designing the seige scene had its difficulties because I wanted the soldiers with their cannon in the foreground, and also a long enough view to show the Cathedral spire being shattered. In fact design overcame ballistics, as I have been assured that from the angle of my cannon it would have been impossible to hit the central spire! I do hope you will all forgive me.

The Eighteenth Century Embroidery Details

This is the only central motif not worked directly onto the canvas. Because of the fineness of the portraits, these were worked on 22 count canvas and then appliquéd into position.

Embroidering portraits is an entirely different discipline to painting faces. when you paint, you are standing back from your work and you can see immediately whether you have the brush strokes right. With embroidery you are working much closer and you cannot see the impression you are creating until you have put enough stitches in and take an arm's length view. Twice Boulton was cross-eyed before I got him right!

Another triumph, I felt, was Shugborough Hall - with all those windows and columns. I used 28 count canvas and it took ten days to design and another two weeks to execute.

The Eighteenth Century

Kings and Queens of the Century

Anne reigned 1702-1714. The last monarch of the Stuart dynasty. She was the sister of Queen Mary II. Married Prince George of Denmark but left no heirs.

George I reigned 1714-1727. First Hanoverian king. When George's young bride Sophia Dorothea discovered that her husband had a mistress she created a scene and later took a lover herself . Her lack of discretion with Count Koningsmark threatened to ridicule George, Duke of Hanover, so he divorced her and she was forced to live in a remote castle, never seeing her two sons again. As for Koningsmark? Well, whispers that he had been hacked to pieces in Sophia Dorothea's royal apartments were given credence when later renovations to the palace produced human remains.

So the first Hanoverian King offended his English subjects, not only by his lack of inclination to learn their language but - as ever the champion of the underdog, they objected to the way he was treating Sophia Dorothea. Now where have I heard all this going on more recently?

George II reigned 1727-1760. The last English king to lead his troops into battle.

George III reigned 1760-1820. The grandson of George II. He was the first monarch since Queen Anne to be born and educated in England.

The Borders

Anyone who has an early postcard of the eighteenth century panel will find that in the borders there are motifs of a flower, a butterfly and the humble onion. Later, Sylvia replaced these motifs with William Murdock's gas lamp, John Wilkinson's portrait and a moon and telescope representing the Lunar Society.

I have included Murdock and Wilkinson, along with Abraham Darby, later in this section, in the dialogue about those other Captains of Industry, Matthew Boulton and James Watt, so it only remains here to tell you about the Lunar Society.

Formed around 1766, possibly in Dr Erasmus Darwin's Lichfield home, the Lunar Society met each month on the Monday nearest to the full moon so that the 'Lunatics' could expect moonlight for their homeward journey in the early hours of the morning. At these meetings the keenest brains of the Midlands - Matthew Boulton, James Watt, William Murdock, Josiah Wedgwood, Thomas Day, Joseph Priestley and others - gathered to indulge in philosophical arguments and discuss the exciting technological achievements that were advancing the century.

The Panel

The Opening Motif

The white horse of Hanover introduces us to the Hanoverian dynasty.

Queen Anne was the last of the Stuart monarchs and this was in spite of the fact that she endured seventeen pregnancies in an effort to provide the nation with an heir. When, in 1701, her last surviving child, the Duke of Clarence died, an Act of Succession was passed to make sure that the crown did not fall by default onto a Catholic head.

Anne's nearest Protestant relative was a grand-daughter of King James I, Sophia, wife of the Elector of Hanover, and it was her son George who succeeded to the throne in 1714. The new King was not overjoyed about having to leave his homeland to take up his English inheritance and the English were not too impressed when he arrived, totally unable to speak the language and trailing two physically unprepossessing mistresses in his wake. Still, at least he was a Protestant!

In spite of the Act of Succession, the House of Hanover did not find their path to the British throne (including Ireland, American colonies, Caribbean islands, Gibraltar and Minorca) completely uncluttered with the baggage of James II and his Catholic descendants. James Edward, born in the year of his father's 'abdication', came into the world with such a dubious pedigree that a law was passed imposing on the Lord Chamberlain the obligation to attend all future royal births - a prevailing situation until Queen Elizabeth's first child, Prince Charles was born in 1948.

So, not only was the exiled House of Stuart Catholic, but its blood line was in dispute. There were of course still Jacobites - supporters of James II and his heirs, and they carried on causing trouble for the first half of the century. The final effort to recapture the throne was in 1745 when James Edward's son, Bonnie Prince Charlie, landed in Scotland and marched with an army of Highlanders south for London hoping to pick up more fighting men along the way.

By the time he reached Derby it had become apparent that the English were unprepared to fight for his cause. He turned tail for Scotland again, passing back through Leek and the Moorlands which had already suffered the usual looting and marauding at the hands of an army on the march. The village of Okeover did not escape the Pretender's attentions. The church was pillaged and the parson robbed of his silver snuff-box, while at the Hall the servants were threatened with their lives as the Squire's horses were saddled up and ridden away.

Staffordshire raised its first regular regiment of infantry in 1705 to fight in the Wars of the Spanish Succession under Colonel Luke Lillingston, who had just returned from an expedition in the West Indies.

The Colonel almost owned the regiment which bore his name. He received a lump sum payment from the Government - frequently in arrears - and from this he provided the troops with their food, uniform, pay, and sometimes their accommodation.

In 1707 the Regiment was sent to the West Indies, and for some reason, possibly because of the disease ridden, tropical climate, Lillingston declined to accompany his men. The Regiment was put under the command of Lillingston's Lieutenant-Colonel, James Jones, and eventually its name changed to Jones' Regiment.

This naming of a regiment after its commanding officer or officers became unwieldly by the middle of the century, and in 1751 a new system was introduced whereby each regiment was allocated a number based on the year of its founding. Jones's Regiment became the 38th Foot.

After 57 years in the Caribbean, the 38th returned home and were one of the first regiments to be drafted out to America where rumblings of discontent heralded the eventual loss of the North American colonies.

In 1782 it was decided to link the numbered regiments with counties and the 38th was given the title of the 38th Regiment of Foot (First Staffordshire).

The Staffordshire Regimental Museum, located next to their Whittington Barracks between Lichfield and Tamworth, makes an interesting visit. Here I found a little ditty penned by one of Staffordshire's home-sick lads during the First World War:

> When the war has rolled away,
> When the war has rolled away,
> When the German's are forgotten,
> And the Kaiser's dead and rotten,
> Then we'll all go back to Wolverhampton,
> When the war has rolled away.

Samuel Johnson was born 7th September 1709, in the same Lichfield street as Elias Ashmole, and taken that same day across the road to St Mary's church (now the Heritage Centre) for baptism. His father was a bookseller in Lichfield with stalls in Uttoxeter and Ashby-de-la-Zouch markets, a following which never appealed to young Samuel.

In fact, brilliant as Samuel was, he left university without a degree and wandered about aimlessly for several years not quite knowing what to do with himself. Shortly after marrying a widow some years older than himself he decided on a career as a schoolmaster but this was not a success. His school attracted only two or three pupils, one of them David Garrick. Later Johnson and Garrick, both impoverished, set off to see what riches London could offer. Garrick found fame on the stage while Johnson gradually acquired a reputation as a journalist and writer, and in 1747 announced his plan to put together a dictionary.

During the years that Johnson laboured over his dictionary he suffered with continual ill health. His much beloved wife, Tetty, also died. He published the first dictionary of the English language in 1755, eight years after he started the task. A stupendous achievement for one man, especially as he had received little encouragement, interest or support for his project.

In 1763 James Boswell met Johnson and to him we owe the biography of this great man of amusing and provocative sayings. Here's part of Boswell's wonderful description of his companion's shambling appearance:

"His brown suit of clothes looked very rusty; he had on a little, shrivelled, unpowdered wig, which was too small for his head; his shirt neck and knees of his breeches were loose...."

Such disregard for dress was not generally acceptable in the London society where Johnson mixed, but he was indifferent to how he looked, and because people wanted to enjoy his clever wit, they accepted the eccentricity of his appearance.

Although Johnson went home to Lichfield several times, he never actually lived there again and he is buried in Poet's Corner, Westminster Abbey. In Lichfield there is a fine statue of him, his cumbersome frame seated and facing his birthplace. Boswell is there too, standing at the opposite side of the market place.

This century saw medicine move out of the dark ages of superstition into the light of science. The trade of 'barber-surgeon' became the profession of the specialist, smallpox vaccination was discovered by Jenner, and much was done to reduce the appalling mortality rate amongst mothers and their new born babies. Hospitals were founded, mainly by philanthropists, and in 1766 public subscription provided the means for two houses in Foregate Street, Stafford, to be opened as the Staffordshire General Infirmary.

By 1772, an 80 bed hospital was opened, again in Foregate Street, and the following year 184 outpatients were treated. 212 sick people were admitted, of whom 106 were cured, 8 died and 20 were considered as incurable. Twenty years later it was decided that the wash house under the men's ward was bad for the patients' health, and that new facilities should be built. A general tightening of belts was necessary and the meal rations were reduced. Sunday was the only day when meat and fresh vegetables were served; during the week bread, cheese and porridge were the staple diet.

Surgical operations were carried out on the wards until 1808 when a room was fitted out specifically for the purpose, although at this time the trustees still avoided committing themselves to providing baths.

The building, the design of Staffordshire man Benjamin Wyatt of Weeford, finally outlived its usefulness as a hospital in the late twentieth century and has stood empty for several years surrounded by rumours of demolition. The County Council has come under attack at this prospect and it now seems likely that the facade may be preserved to front a modern building.

Staffordshire's sons really started to get to grips with their Counties natural resources this century. Exploitation was the name of the game and the result was great wealth for those who grasped the opportunities literally under their feet.

Lands granted by William the Conqueror to his loyal Barons now provided rich pickings for their descendants. Those newly affluent in Stuart times, who had bought or married their way into the upper classes, the Wards of Dudley for instance, found that their estates could provide far greater incomes than that obtained by farming the land. In some cases even the parks surrounding their magnificent halls became more than status symbols - a vast new source of wealth, coal, lay waiting to be harnessed to the latest technologies and transported by the new turnpiked roads and canals.

At the beginning of the century the roads throughout Staffordshire were totally inadequate for the job of transporting people, raw materials and manufactured goods. One of the reasons for this was that responsibility for road maintenance fell to the parish. The roads leading from industrialised areas in the south of the county such as Walsall, Wednesbury and Dudley, and the Potteries in the north, were subject to continual heavy traffic and the burden of their upkeep was well beyond the fiscal means of parish councils.

The problem was addressed by the introduction of Turnpike Trusts, which empowered interested parties such as industrialists and manufacturers, to take over a stretch of road, repair and maintain it, and charge a fee to the users. The London to Carlisle Road between Darlaston-on-Stowe and Talke was the first to be turnpiked in Staffordshire, and twelve years later, in 1729, the Birmingham to Wednesbury Road followed. Later in the century, Josiah Wedgwood took responsibility for turnpiking much of the Potteries to enable his wares to be transported further afield.

Thus, slowly - for turnpiking was not the success it could have been if more of the operators had been interested in providing good roads instead of fat toll receipts - the packhorse gave way to the wagon, and Staffordshire began to trade on more profitable terms with the rest of the Country.

Better roads also brought in swifter and more comfortable personal travel by way of the stagecoach. In Queen Anne's reign a coach tugged along by six horses could progress at no more than walking pace; 50 years later passengers were carried along more swiftly by lighter, more comfortable coaches, drawn by four horses. Such a coach was the Red Rover which ran daily between Birmingham and Stafford.

But the transport revolution did not stop at turnpiking. The Shire's industrialists were very much aware that in other parts of England river transport was faster, cheaper and more efficient than road carriage and so various schemes were attempted to make our shallow inland waterways serviceable thoroughfares. There was only limited

success in this sphere and the main beneficiaries were without doubt the Burton Brewers. With the improved navigability of the Trent they were able to ship beer to the Baltic via Hull and boast Empress Catherine as a customer.

The answer to the problem came in the form of a semi-literate Staffordshire millwright from Leek named James Brindley. While still an apprentice in Macclesfield, he delighted his employer with a natural talent for making and mending machines. Eventually Brindley started his own engineering firm in Mill Street, Leek. He constructed a flint grinding mill for Josiah and Thomas Wedgwood in 1758.

Later, this somewhat eccentric genius, who retired to bed to solve his engineering problems and never made any written plans, was to collaborate with the Wedgwood potters again. Josiah Wedgwood was one of the main protagonists at the public meeting held in 1765 to establish the feasibility of building the first canal in Staffordshire, to link the Trent with the Mersey. Brindley, although of limited education, was able to describe his plans with exceptional lucidity and he inspired the promoters with his Grand Trunk Canal scheme - a plan for a main artery with other canals linking to it. The 93 mile (146 kilometre) Grand Trunk was started in 1766 and took eleven years to fully complete, mainly due to the length of time needed to build the 1³/₄ mile (2.82 kilometre) long Harecastle tunnel north of the potteries.

While this great construction was under way, Brindley was also providing an outlet to Bristol and the south-west, via the Staffordshire-Worcestershire canal. He then cut a much needed branch from Birmingham to Aldersley near Wolverhampton which wound a tortuous 22 mile route through Smethwick, Tipton, Coseley and Bilston calling at as many ironworks and coal pits as possible along the way. The area through which it ran was heavily industrialised, although it is interesting to note that a contemporary map (1772) shows Ocker Hill at Tipton still to be heavily wooded.

Canals were the way forward and by the end of the century man-made water courses criss-crossed Staffordshire providing the County with the cheap, efficient, wholesale transport that helped the Industrial Revolution to surge ahead.

The Wedgwoods, alongside the Adams, had been making pots in Burslem since the fifteenth century. Josiah Wedgwood was born in 1730 at the Churchyard Works, Burslem, the youngest of Thomas and Mary Wedgwood's twelve children. When Thomas died in 1739, Josiah's schooling came to an abrupt end as his eldest brother insisted he joined the family business.

After serving his apprenticeship Josiah joined forces for a time with another potter Thomas Whieldon at Fenton where he started to make meticulous records of his experiments. In 1759 he began his own business and perfected the successful formula for a cream-coloured earthenware which was not only pleasing to the eye, but sturdy enough to 'bear sudden alterations of heat and cold'. Queen Charlotte, the wife of George III, ordered a tea and coffee service in the new ivory clay and was so satisfied that she allowed Josiah to give it the name 'Queen's Ware.'

With success behind him, Josiah bought a 350 acre estate and built a new factory, along with houses for his workers, a school and a chapel. He called the new village Etruria and to celebrate the official opening he personally threw six basalt vases, four of which survived the firing process to became known as the 'First Day's Vase'. Sylvia has included Josiah with his First Day's Vase in what she calls her 'portrait gallery of eighteenth century giants'.

And indeed, poorly educated Josiah was a giant of his time. He was a master potter who gave us Black Basalt and Jasper stoneware. He was a philanthropist who gave his workers decent homes, welfare and education. He was an ardent campaigner for the abolition of slavery. He was a thrusting businessman who formed the General Chamber of Manufacturers of Great Britain, an organisation with a voice loud enough to influence government policy. He was an entrepreneur who campaigned for better transport routes out of the Midlands, particularly the Trent-Mersey canal which ran past his Etruria manufactory, and for which, in July 1766 he cut the first sod.

B ottle kilns such as those depicted next to Wedgwood and his First Day's Vase, were in use until the middle of the twentieth century as the principal method of firing the potter's wares. Their name derives from the distinctive shape of the external structure which preserved heat and protected the internal kiln, and they were the predominant feature of the Potteries landscape along with a black pall of smoke.

Sadly, none of Wedgwood's Bottle kilns have survived, but at the Wedgwood Visitor Centre at Barlaston you can see a model interior showing how the pottery was encased in 'saggers' and stacked ready for firing. For those interested in the real thing, Gladstone Pottery Museum at Longton have preserved five bottle kilns and have a complete, up-and-running, factory much of which is in Grade 2 listed buildings.

Three more from Sylvia's portrait gallery, Matthew Boulton, James Watt and John Wilkinson must take their share of the blame for having turned most of the southern tip of Staffordshire from barren heath into a densely populated, disease and despair ridden, industrial hell hole.

Perhaps this is a little harsh on them, because, as we have already seen, Staffordshire had been gradually industrialising since medieval times. However, once Boulton and Watt teamed up with Wilkinson to harness steam power there was nothing gradual about the technological achievements of the next fifty years, dubbed by history the Industrial Revolution.

With the natural deposits of iron ore as raw material, coal as fuel, limestone as flux and fireclay for building the furnaces, the means for the Revolution were all there under the surface of the Staffordshire soil just waiting for the technology to come along. Probably the first of these latter day techno-gurus was Abraham Darby, born at Wrens Nest in Dudley. In 1709 he discovered how to smelt ore with coal instead of charcoal. Dud Dudley, (one of eleven illegitimate children of the Lord Dudley who sold out to Humble Ward in the 1600s) reckoned he had made the coal-into-coke discovery. This boast seems to be supported by the coke slag from his Himley furnace, but, in any event, it was Darby who perfected the technique and gave the housewife affordable cooking pots.

As the demand for iron grew (there was always somebody, somewhere wanting cannon and other weaponry not to mention the domestic market that flowed from the improved, cheaper iron castings), the requirement for coal likewise increased. With the call for extra coal came the urgent need for some kind of pump to keep the mines free from flooding, an ever present problem for coalmasters who lived with the constant threat of flooded mines and bankruptcy.

So, hot on the trail of Abraham Darby's breakthrough came Thomas Newcomen with the first steam engine in 1711. This engine was installed at a coal mine in Coneygre near Tipton for Lord Dudley and Ward, the great-grandson of Humble Ward.

These two inventions - coke smelting and steam power, provided much of the impetus for the improvement in transportation discussed earlier. So, by the middle of the century the scene was set for Boulton, Watt and Wilkinson to combine their multiple talents - and in Boulton's case his wife's fortune, and hurl us full tilt into the next frenzied stages of human advancement.

Matthew Boulton was the son of a toymaker - the name used to describe the manufacture of small, metal fancy goods. He was married at St Mary's church Lichfield to a local heiress Anne Robinson, who came with a dowry of £28,000. This windfall gave Matthew the opportunity to purchase barren land in Handsworth (in Staffordshire until 1911) where the Soho manufactory was built in 1775 at a cost of £9,000. The Soho Works were innovative in that they were purpose built with the capacity to employ vast numbers of people - more than a thousand eventually worked there. Thus the shift began from the domestic workshop to the factory era.

Aware of the urgent need to improve upon Newcomen's sixty year old steam engine, Boulton joined forces in 1774 with a young Scottish mathematical instrument maker, named James Watt, to develop a universal power source. Watt's modified steam engine needed an accurately bored cylinder and it was to John Wilkinson that he now turned.

About three years ago, the Black Country Bugle published a photograph of three women, Sheila, Irene and Mary who were sending good wishes to Darlaston friends left behind years ago when they emigrated to Australia. I was intrigued. Born and bred in West Bromwich I can remember the arguments with my Black Country father over a ten o'clock curfew and I just could not understand how these three 'wenches' had persuaded their Darlaston dads to let them go to Australia. So I wrote and asked them, and not wishing to appear crassly nosey, I sent them one of my published magazine stories and left them to believe that perhaps I wanted the information as background material for a future story. Within weeks I received a bulky parcel with a letter from Sheila Wilkinson explaining that she and her two friends were all married women before they went to Australia. The parcel? Well that was her husband Geoff's manuscript - the biography of his distant forebear John Wilkinson, laboriously researched over thirty years from the other side of the globe, and now finished and ready for publication. But the Aussies didn't want to know! As I was a 'real writer' Sheila's letter said, would I look it over and give my comments?

The book is now under consideration with the editor of the Blackcountryman Magazine and in the meantime, Geoff agreed to condense his three hundred page manuscript into a 400 word potted history of his world famous predecessor, so over to you, Geoff:

John Wilkinson's father was the ironmaster who invented 'a box iron with which laundresses could smooth fine linen' for which my wife has never forgiven me. John himself was a brilliant inventor and engineer, and is one of the founding fathers of the industrial revolution, British engineering and industry in general.

He established his ironworks at Bradley near Bilston where he introduced the use of coke-smelting. He manufactured cannons which were bored with the world's first accurate boring machine that he invented. This stopped the cannon bursting when fired. With these reliable weapons Britain's army and navy could put her enemies to flight, but I'm sorry to have to say that John sent his younger brother, William to France to produce the same military hardware for Napoleon!

The machine that produced these cannon was able to bore the cylinder for James Watt's steam engine, the great invention which put the industrial revolution into top gear.

His enthusiasm for all things made from iron earned John the nickname 'Iron Mad Wilkinson'. He was even buried in an iron coffin and tried to convince others to do the same. He had his coffin made several years before his death and kept it in the house so that he could show it to visitors.

It was prophesied by a gypsy whose palm he refused to cross, that after his death he would be buried five times, a prophesy that was to come true. His showpiece coffin proved too small and so he had to be temporarily interred while a new one was cast. Then on the way to his final resting place at Castlehead, his home near Grange-over-Sands, he was accidentally buried in the mud while crossing the estuary at low tide as his bearers tried to take a short cut, and remained there until he could be dug out. The hole cut in the rock at Castlehead that was to form his tomb had been cut to accommodate his original coffin and was too small for the new one, so he was temporarily interred again while this was enlarged. Later the house was sold and so his remains were removed from the tomb and buried under the floor of St Paul's church at Lindale-in-Cartmel where he remains to this day.

It might be said of him that even in death he was larger than life and no other member of our family has ever been able to claim that distinction.

Geoff Wilkinson, late of Darlaston, now Victor Harbor, South Australia. 12th August 1999

By the way, Sheila asked me to mention that before she married Geoff her name was Baggot (though spelt with two g's) and that her family kept goats for centuries.

Another of Sylvia's giants - although he did not get a portrait because of the shortage of space, was William Murdock who, like Watt, came from Scotland. Sylvia particularly wanted to feature him because she feels that he is something of an unsung hero overshadowed by the achievements of his employers. He had been working with locomotion in Cornwall where he frightened the villagers with his noisy experiments, and Boulton recalled him to the Soho Works where he turned his talents to the invention of coal gas lighting in 1792. Ten years later his work made gas lighting a practicable, commercial proposition and the exterior of the Soho Works was the first to enjoy artificial illumination.

Admiral George Anson came from a family who started the social climb in the late Tudor years. By the early 17th century William Anson from Dunston, who had married Joan Whitehall from Oldbury, was a barrister of Lincoln's Inn and successful enough to buy the Shugborough estate. These lands had, before the reformation shake-up, belonged to the Bishop of Lichfield. William's grandson began the stately home of Shugborough shown in Sylvia's vignette and two of his sons also left their mark for posterity. Thomas, the elder, inherited his father's estate and the fine square, three storey house he had built; while George went to sea. Thomas encouraged the arts, collaborated with Brindley and Wedgwood on a number of industrial projects, became Member of Parliament for Lichfield and roamed the eastern Mediterranean in search of ideas and artefacts for his Shugborough home.

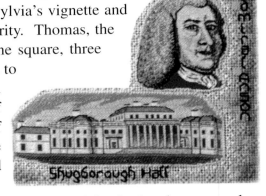

Shugborough Hall

George's naval career was long and spectacular. He joined when he was twelve and nearly half a century later when he was sixty, he put to sea to lead a successful blockade of Brest during one of the interminable French Wars. In 1740 he was given a squadron of six ships and sent to the Pacific to attack Spanish possessions. It was a gruelling, four year voyage in which he circumnavigated the world and spent three months battling round Cape Horn in continuous storms. At last, with only his flag ship left afloat, he arrived home - but he did have a captured Spanish treasure ship laden with a £400,000 cargo in his wake. He was made a baron and appointed to the Board of Admiralty where he did much to remodel the Navy and established the corps of Marines. He had married but there were no children to leave his share of the Spanish spoils to, so he helped his brother Thomas with the enlargement of Shugborough Hall.

After the Admiral's death, Thomas inherited his brother's fortune and so was able to continue apace with the beautification of his hall and park. Enlarging the park meant moving the village of Shugborough lock, stock and barrel. The villagers did well enough out of the move though, for they were rehoused in modern homes in Great Haywood, now a pretty village with the longest pack-horse bridge in England.

In the next century another Thomas was made a Viscount and his son was created Earl of Lichfield. When the 4th Earl died in 1960 the estate was offered to the Treasury in lieu of death duties and ultimately transferred to the National Trust, though the 5th Earl, Lord Patrick Lichfield, still lives there at least part of the year.

The monks of Burton Abbey have been credited with the discovery that water filtered through the local gypsum produced a superior ale, but I cannot help thinking that the locals would have discovered this elixir well before the thirteenth century. The sparseness of the population and the lack of communication in those early days would have ensured that the knowledge did not

Town House of Wm. Bass

founder of Bass Brewery Burton 1777

travel. Certainly, at the dissolution in 1545 when the Abbey Estates and Brew House were passed to Sir William Paget, Burton ales were 'noted for their excellence'. By then there were many small inns and alehouses in the town who were selling the liquor, and it was also supplied in casks to the local gentry. Hence the ease with which it was conveyed to Mary Queen of Scotts while she was a prisoner at Tutbury Castle. (see 16th century).

However, brewing was not truly commercial until early in the 18th century when the first merchant brewers appeared, and William Bass was not even born when these men, including William Worthington, started trading.

William Bass was, in fact, a carrier when he decided to set up a brewery in Burton and made it his pledge to use only the finest barley and hops along with the area's mineral-laden well waters. Although William died ten years later, his son carried on brewing and developed a thriving export business with Germany, Finland and Russia using the deepened River Trent as his outlet to the coast via Hull. Incredibly, because of the appalling state of the roads in England at the time, this lengthy journey proved a cheaper option than selling in the home market.

The Closing Motif

The loss of the American colonies in the reign of George III seems an apt closing motif as it was certainly the end of an era. The signing of the Declaration of Independence in 1776 threw up an amazing quirk of fate that earned one man an enduring place in Staffordshire's history and a windfall for a Wolverhampton school. Button Gwinnett hailed from Gloucestershire. He moved to Wolverhampton where he married a local girl in St Peter's church and subsequently his three daughters were baptised there. He traded in the town, became a pillar of local society and a governor of the Blue Coat School. Then, in 1765 the Gwinnetts emigrated to Savannah, in Georgia.

The family settled well in their adopted country. Button worked diligently, prospered financially and was elected to Congress. In 1776 he saw his finest hour when he was one of the 55 signatories on the Declaration of Independence. The following year he was killed in a duel. A few years later, when people started collecting the signatures of the 55 Congressmen who had signed the Declaration of Independence, Button Gwinnett's was by far the rarest.

By the end of the century Button's autograph was already fetching £500. Then, here in Staffordshire, someone clearing out old files found that in 1761 Button had attended three meetings of subscribers to Wolverhampton Blue Coat School and signed the minutes. These three signatures caused a flutter on both sides of the Atlantic and left the Bluecoat School the better off by over £10,000.

The Nineteenth Century

Kings and Queens of the Century

George IV ('Prinny') reigned 1820-1830 although he had been Regent since 1811. One child Charlotte who died in childbirth.

William IV reigned 1830-1837. George's brother. His two legitimate daughters died in infancy. He also had ten illegitimate children.

Queen Victoria reigned from 1837-1901 making her Britain's longest reigning monarch. She inherited the throne from her uncle when she was just eighteen years old. She married Prince Albert of Saxe-Coburg-Gotha and because of the strategically arranged royal marriages of their nine children, Victoria became known as the Grandmother of Europe. She was the last of the Hanoverian rulers.

The borders

The natural flora and fauna has disappeared completely from the borders now to make way for some of the County's early football teams. Football, of a sort, was already being played when William the Conqueror arrived and even though Edward III, in the fourteenth century, instructed his sheriffs to suppress it - he felt that his subjects would be better employed practising their arrow shooting skills - the game of football persisted.

The introduction of work-free Saturday afternoons in the middle of this century was the first time in industrial society that the working man had enjoyed leisure time plus a little money above that required to exist. It was the catalyst from which organised, professional football swiftly emerged.

Many of the original football teams were church based. Urban district clergy were aware that their flocks were living under every sort of handicap - poor food, lack of sanitation, cramped housing, and even with Saturday afternoons off, appallingly long hours. They knew that exercise would be beneficial to these people and so during the 1870s and 1880s they encouraged regulated football games and often the vicar himself would be a team member.

Other clubs were formed by drinking companions at the local pub while many teams were organised by youths working together in a factory. The Wolverhampton Wanderers were formed when some young pupil-teachers were encouraged by the headmaster to put a team together. St Lukes School, Blakenhall, played on a piece of rough ground off Goldthorn Hill and their records go right the way back to 10th November 1876 when, at a meeting held at the school, interested parties were invited to form a football team. The Goldthorn Football Club came into being and the headmaster, Harry Barcroft presented its members with a ball. The team's first competitive match was played on 13th January 1877 against local railway employees known as Stafford FC who already enjoyed something of a reputation. Harry Barcroft played in goal on that historic occasion and the new team were beaten 8 - 0.

The fledgling players weren't unduly put off by this defeat and during the next four seasons their game improved to such an extent that they were able to trounce their opponents with such scores as 17 - 0 against Whitmore Reans, and 15 - 0 against Graiseley. The team amalgamated with the Blakenhall Wanderers Cricket Club and adopted the name Wolverhampton Wanderers Football Club - and 'The Wolves' as they are popularly known were one of the original six northern sides invited to join the Football League in 1888.

On 23rd March 1888, representatives from Stoke, West Bromwich Albion and Wolverhampton Wanderers attended a meeting along with nominees from a few other clubs to discuss the feasibility of forming a league that would guarantee a definite list of games described as a 'fixity of fixtures'. From this meeting the Football League came into being with its twelve founder members - six from Lancashire and six from the Midlands.

Stoke (who didn't add 'City' until 1925) boast of a team back in 1863, although evidence is scant, and popular legend seems to have more to do with it than substantiated fact. There is no doubt about a foundation date of 1868 though, when Stoke Railway Works were instrumental in forming the Stoke Ramblers. The 'Ramblers' tag soon disappeared, leaving them simply as Stoke by the time they were invited to join the Football League. Unfortunately the questionable honour of being the first team to lose their place in the Football League went to Stoke, who finished bottom in the second season 1889/90. They regained their place after just one season although it took them almost a hundred more to actually win the League Cup (1992). Sylvia has formed her cameo by picking out the crest from the top of their shield.

When the Trent and Mersey canal was being built in the late 18th century, a series of wharves, factories and villages mushroomed along its tow-paths near to Burslem and the area became known as the 'Port Vale'. About a hundred years later this name was adopted by an athletics club formed primarily to play cricket. It seems that the Port Vale Athletics Club soon became involved in football as mention was given in the Staffordshire Sentinel of 16th October 1880 of Port Vale FC.

There is a popularly supported theory for an origination date four years earlier in 1876 but this lacks anything definite in the way of proof except for the intriguing fact that in 1926 the club held a jubilee celebration.

Their first games were played on the Port Vale meadows, but by 1881 local publicans had provided them with a proper ground which enabled them to make an admission charge. Although they trounced the English Cup semi-finalists Derby Junction with a score of 10 - 0 their record for the 1887/8 season did not gain them inclusion into the Football League.

West Bromwich Albion (the youngest of Sylvia's five Staffordshire teams, if we give the benefit to Port Vale and Stoke), know exactly how and when they came into existence. It was one Saturday afternoon in September 1879 when the youths of George Salter Spring Works, at the top end of West Bromwich, decided to copy their mates in Wednesbury and start a football team.

A committee was formed and an obstacle immediately loomed into view. As no one in the area played the game, there wasn't a football to be bought in any local shop. So the committee members, each having stumped up sixpence, walked to Wednesbury where the necessary equipment was purchased. Perhaps the team's first name, West Bromwich Strollers originated from this journey to acquire a ball!

Two seasons later they adopted the name Albion (a West Bromwich area) in place of Strollers and in 1888 they were invited to become founder members of the Football League. The club has two nicknames. 'The Baggies' perhaps arose because during their early days they used to pass a bag round amongst the spectators for donations, or another explanation, one I seem to remember my grandfather telling me, is simply that they wore baggy shorts.

The thrush or throstle, though rare in West Bromwich by the time I was growing up there in the 1940s, was common enough for the team to adopt the bird as their emblem, so they also became known as The Throstles.

There were many loosely formed football clubs in Walsall during the 1870s including St Matthew's Church Institute, Bott Lane Mission, Walsall Albion and the first team ever to be recorded in the town, back in 1873, Victoria Swifts.

In 1874 another club was formed, the Walsall Town Football Club and for its inaugural game - which was against Rushall, so many eager Walsall players turned up that it was decided to play fifteen-a-side and to loan surplus Walsall players to the Rushall team. Rushall won 3 - 1 with one of their goals being scored by a 'loaned' Walsall player.

By the end of the 1874-75 season two Walsall teams had emerged as reliable and regularly playing sides, Walsall Town fielding fifteen players and The Swifts fielding twelve. These two teams attracted crowds of up to 3500 with such scores as 17- 0 Town v Willenhall, and 19 - 0 Swifts v Nettlefolds Athletic. Between themselves, too, there was rivalry, and both teams played in the 1882 English Cup (the original 'Football Association Cup').

The two clubs eventually amalgamated and became the Walsall Town Swifts and in the summer of 1892 Walsall became one of the founder members of the newly-formed Football League Division Two. The name The Saddlers which has become something more than a nick name to the club came about because of Walsall's connection with the equestrian leather trade.

2 0,000 miles of wire were made to form the core of the first Atlantic cable at Thomas Bolton's copper works at Oakamoor in the Churnet Valley. The contract was begun in 1857 and each mile of the cable core weighed 90 lb (41kilo) and cost £5 to manufacture. The following year the first telegraphic messages were relayed along the cable and 732 communications were flashed between the two continents before the line failed and remained mute for ever more. It was another seven years before the next, more successful cable, was laid.

There was no effective civilian police force in England until Sir Robert Peel introduced his blue-coated, top-hatted, truncheon-armed 'bobbies' in 1829.

The Police Act of 1839 enabled counties to set up their own forces and in Staffordshire the Act was adopted in 1842. The County was split into the Pottery Police District, the Mining Police District and the Rural Police District all under the control of a Chief Constable whose annual salary was £350 plus £100 travelling expenses.

The Potteries, with a population of 70,000, was allocated four superintendents to regulate 60 constables whose wages ranged from 16 to 20 shillings a week. One superintendent was given sufficient pay to include the upkeep of a horse. The Mining District, in effect the Black Country (although that name had not yet been coined) with a population of 100,000, was allocated six superintendents and 90 constables. Two superintendents were paid sufficient to keep a horse each. The Rural area was covered by eight superintendents, each allocated sufficient salary for the maintenance of a horse.

Perhaps our first 'bobbies' were apt to be boorish, for in regulations issued circa 1859, constables were instructed that when walking along the streets 'it was particularly desirable that they should not shoulder foot passengers, but give way in a mild manner.'

T he wives and daughters of wealthy Victorian men occupied much of their time with embroidery. They talked about it, read articles about it and travelled to exhibitions to see it. Elizabeth Wardle, the wife of a wealthy silk manufacturer in Leek, was such a lady, and in 1879, encouraged by William Morris, she formed the Leek Embroidery Society so that she and her companions could benefit from their shared knowledge. They had many designs drawn for them by famous Victorian artists, including Walter Crane, Gerald Horsley and Morris himself.

Some years later the ladies undertook to embroider a faithful facsimile of the Bayeux tapestry - all 230 feet of it. The work was a great success at exhibitions throughout England, and in Germany and America. Unfortunately, with carriage costs and other expenses, the tours made little money and towards the end of the century the tapestry was offered to the town of Leek, who declined it, and was then sold to Alderman Arthur Hill, as a gift to the people of Reading, to commemorate the time when he had been their mayor. He paid £300 for it and today it is permanently housed in the Reading Museum. Very occasionally the tapestry has returned home to Leek, the last time in 1984 to mark its centenary. Alderman Hill was so much more far-sighted than his contemporaries in Leek - I hope and trust that the people of Staffordshire will cherish this gift of Sylvia's, or perhaps like the people of Leek they may lose it.

The Panel

The Opening Motif

S ylvia introduced the Marquis of Anglesey's ancestors in the 16th century, when William Paget, son of a Wednesbury nailer, was Lord Chancellor to Henry VIII and nicely placed to partake of the spoils during the Dissolution. We left him an upwardly mobile Tudor baron with interests in politics, agriculture and industry. The family prospered over the next 250 years and the 7th Baron was created Earl of Uxbridge. Henry, the 11th Earl, was commander of the horse artillery and cavalry at Waterloo and during the battle he was riding with the Duke of Wellington when a cannon ball shattered his leg. Legend says the following conversation took place:

Earl: "Good God, Sir, my leg's blown off."

Duke: "I'm damned if it isn't."

Whether you believe that or not is entirely up to you, though the rest of the story probably has more substance. It tells us that the Earl was taken to a draper's shop in Waterloo where the remainder of the leg was amputated - without anaesthetic - and buried in the tradesman's garden with a weeping willow to mark the spot. Paget was the first man to be fitted with an artificial leg which bent at the knee and this limb is now a family heirloom. Shortly after the Battle of Waterloo the Earl was created Marquis of Anglesey for his services to King and Country.

As I mentioned in the 18th century, the Burton brewers were trading with Russia and so they faced a serious financial problem when the Napoleonic Wars caused the Baltic ports to be closed to them.

Another avenue of trade was opening up in India, which the British were colonising. The administrators, their families and thousands of soldiers were enduring the torrid Indian climate and they called for a beer that would slake their thirst. A new pale ale, light, sparkling and pleasantly bitter was brewed to meet this special requirement. It was immediately successful and restored Bass's flagging fortunes. It seems that there was no particular intention to introduce the East India Pale Ale onto the home market until a shipwreck in the Irish Sea caused a fortuitous backlash for Michael Bass, who had inherited the business from his father. 300 casks were salvaged and auctioned off in Liverpool to pay the underwriters' costs. These casks found their way all over the country and wherever it was tasted, the India Pale Ale met with eager acclaim. Suddenly Michael found himself with a healthy home market for his new brew.

Michael Bass died in 1827 and his 28 year old son, Michael Thomas Bass the second, inherited the business and turned it into the greatest brewing organisation in the world. He was quick to realise the potential once the railways appeared, and at its peak, Bass had 16 miles of track within the brewery, 11 engines and over 400 wagons. Not only did Michael make use of the railways, he actively championed the cause of the railway workers and helped

found the first railwaymen's union. He also represented Derby in Parliament for 33 years earning himself the venerable title of Father of the House. His youngest brother married Anne Worthington, thus linking the two great brewing families of Burton.

The canals built during the second half of the 1700s were, fifty years later, failing to cope with the increased traffic that their own success had brought and they were also in need of modernisation. This was especially true of Brindley's Birmingham to Wolverhampton canal. In 1829 Thomas Telford, the 'new kid on the block' as far as canal technology was concerned, straightened the waterway by cutting out

seven miles of its length and reduced the number of locks from 30 to 24. Roebuck Lane, the road between West Bromwich and Smethwick, was carried over a new 70 ft (21m) deep cutting by a huge cast-iron structure, the Galton Bridge named after the Galton family who had considerable influence in the area at that time.

Fly boats for passengers were working between Birmingham and Wolverhampton during this period and there is an anecdote about a Frenchman who, even though the locals shouted an alert to him, injured his head by poking it out of the cabin window as they passed a Smethwick bridge. He complained "When you do say 'look out', you do mean 'look in.'"

Galton Bridge was built at the former Horseley Iron Company in Great Bridge, Tipton, and with its span of 154 feet (47m) it was the longest canal bridge in the world. But 'Th'Osley' as the company was known to Black Country folk when I was a girl, was well used to heavy engineering 'firsts', for it was here that the SS Aaron Manby, the world's first iron steam ship was built in 1820. A ship made in Tipton? You can't get any further from the sea than Tipton!

Well, this ship, which was named after one of the firm's partners, was dismantled and sent by canal to London where it was reassembled and subjected to trials on the River Thames. These trials caused great excitement as the Aaron Manby was propelled by revolving steam oars which provided the boat with excellent manoeuvrability. An enthusiastic newspaper report described the oars as 'the most perfect piece of mechanism that has yet been adopted in steam boats'. After her trials, the Aaron Manby sailed to France and spent most of her working life freighting on the Seine. She is believed to have been broken up in France, in 1855.

Staffordshire produced its fair share of talented authors and poets during this century and Sylvia acknowledges them with a shelf full of hefty tomes supported against a book-end in the shape of a high-glaze, china Staffordshire dog. I well remember these wretched dogs from my girlhood because there was not a Black Country grandmother's parlour without one.

Arnold Bennett was born in 1867 in Burslem. Although Bennett left the Potteries to live in London when he was twenty one, he never forgot the area's hardships and his books Clayhanger, Anna of the Five Towns and Hilda Lessways, amongst others, give a picture of Potteries life at the end of the 19th century including graphic detail of the wretched plight of young children working in the pottery factories.

Sir Henry Newbolt was born at St Mary's Vicarage Bilston in 1862, and attended, for a short time, Queen Mary's Grammar School. He gave us Drakes Drum and Vitae Lampada, and I wonder if there is any pre-War pupil out there who didn't have to learn 'There's a breathless hush in the close tonight.....'

Jerome K Jerome was born in 1859. He was a prolific writer, but Three Men in a Boat is the book which earned him a plaque on the wall of his birthplace in Walsall. His second Christian name, Klapka was given to him in honour of an exiled Hungarian general who visited the family. Jerome's parents seemed to have a fancy for unusual names - they called one of his sisters Blandina!

The County also produced its fair share of rogues, felons and murderers during the century. Probably the most infamous of these was Dr William Palmer. Certainly the people of Rugeley thought so when shortly after his execution they approached the Prime Minister asking that they be allowed to change the name of their town. Permission was sanctioned by the Prime Minister on condition that they called

their town after him - he was Lord Palmerston ('ton' is Anglo-Saxon for town). I think this story deserves as big a question mark as Paget's leg!

Palmer was born in 1824 and educated locally. He was apprenticed to a firm of druggists in Liverpool and then returned to Rugeley to set up in business. Now Palmer liked a bet on the horses, but unfortunately for him - and other people as it turned out, his lucky streak was as non-existent as his business acumen and he soon found his business failing and his debts mounting. In 1854 his wife, whom he had insured for £13,000 died with alarming suddenness, and within a year his brother, also insured for

£13,000 died. A suspicious insurance company refused to pay out on this second death and later a law was introduced which made it impossible to take out a life assurance contract on the life of another person unless there was an 'insurable interest'.

When Palmer's wealthy racehorse owner-cum-bookmaker friend, John Parsons Cook, died mysteriously, questions started being asked and the police, alerted to the rumblings of suspicion, wanted some answers. Had Palmer practised his poisoning techniques on his neighbours pigs who had all suddenly died? What had happened to his illegitimate daughter and to four of his five other children? What had caused both his wealthy mother-in-law and a family friend to die while staying at his home? And, of course, what had killed his wife and his brother?

By the time thirty two year old Palmer was arrested the locals were ready to lynch him and in the interests of a fair trial, with an impartial jury, the case was removed to the Old Bailey, thus setting a precedent for similar cases.

Palmer did not expect to be convicted as the prosecution couldn't identify the poison he had supposedly used and he was visibly staggered when the 'guilty' verdict was announced. The execution was carried out at Stafford Gaol on June 14th 1856 and was attended by 30,000 spectators, many having made a day trip of the event, arriving from London by special excursion in one of the century's most spectacular inventions, the steam railway train.

Sylvia was desperately short of space on this panel and could not think how to fit in the 1825 opening of Wolverhampton Race Course, or the old coaching house at Hednesford, the Cross Keys, where Palmer incidentally had spent much time watching bare knuckle fighters training. As the debts which had driven Palmer to murder were gambling related, she resolved her design dilemma by including the racecourse, the Cross Keys coaching inn and the prize fighters alongside his portrait.

Public executions, which, as Palmer's turn-out proves, were enormously popular, finally became outlawed twelve years later in 1868. Thereafter Stafford Gaol hanged its miscreants in a more private and less festive atmosphere, with the last execution taking place on 10th March 1914.

Now I have to digress from the panel for a few words. Carl Chinn recently interviewed Sylvia and myself on his radio show and Carl told Sylvia that she could not possibly leave out William Perry the Tipton Slasher. Well, if Sylvia keeps altering the panels I will never get this book to the publisher - there have already been several pieces of flora unpicked from the borders and reworked, the shields of two ancient families, the de Trumwyn's of Cannock and the Wastney's of Colton have vanished, and the famine scene of the 14th century was scrapped to make way for the Whittington Inn. I've had to say "Please, Sylvia, no more changes"; so to the people of Tipton, although Sylvia has neither the time or the space to include Perry, I'll give him a mention here in the century of his birth:

The Tipton Slasher: William Perry 1819-1880. Champion prize fighter of England 1850 to 1857 (and ancestor of Carl Chinn).   Okay Carl?

Although we had our sinners here in Staffordshire, we had our saints too and Walsall have always kept a place in their hearts for Sister Dora.

Dorothy Wyndlow Pattison was born in Richmond, Yorkshire in 1832, the daughter of a clergyman. She volunteered to nurse in the Crimea but her father forbade her to go. Later she joined the Sisterhood of the Good Samaritans and she was sent to nurse at the newly opened Cottage Hospital in Walsall where she immediately caught smallpox. This brush with the dreaded disease gave her the immunity to cope with later outbreaks and in 1868 she visited stricken patients in their homes as the Cottage Hospital had not the facilities to care for them all. By the time the next outbreak occurred, an isolation hospital had been built, but there was no one to nurse the patients. Sister Dora volunteered again and she stayed at the hospital for six months without contact from the outside world other than a daily doctor's visit.

No sooner was the smallpox epidemic over, and Sister Dora reinstalled at her hospital, than a boiler explosion at the Birchills Ironworks threw her back to a situation where she was forced to work long hours with little support. Seventeen men were showered with molten iron and their injuries were so horrific that some of the local ladies who turned up at the Cottage Hospital to assist were unable to face the task and went home. During the next ten days Sister Dora toiled almost without rest making the injured as comfortable as the limited medication of the 1870s would allow.

Sister Dora died three years later at the age of forty six. She had lived and worked amongst the poor of Walsall for less than fifteen years and yet she carved a place in their hearts that has survived for more than a century. The embroidered motif represents the white Sicilian marble statue of Sister Dora unveiled at Walsall eight years after her death. In a panel so heavily charged with success, commercialism and prosperity, Sylvia felt that a reminder of Sister Dora's work amongst poverty and ignorance would help to bring into focus the heavy price that industrialisation cost the people who lived and worked in its environs.

Had Palmer's execution been just two decades sooner it would not have been so well attended. During the years that he was growing up, great minds were developing the steam engine which was to revolutionise people transportation and change for ever the parochial confines of even the poorest in the land. In 1837, the year that Queen Victoria acceded to her throne, the Grand Junction Railway opened, linking Birmingham with Liverpool via the area that was later to be known as the Black

Country, and Stafford. The next year this line was extended south to provide a link with Birmingham through to London.

The descendants of the navvies, who had dug out the miles of waterways across Staffordshire the previous century, now turned their brawny talents to laying railway track for the entrepreneurs who were quick to recognise locomotion as a new solution to the ever increasing freight problem. The massive passenger travel market had not been initially apparent to these speculators, although they were quick to provide services once they realised that the demand was there. New railway companies sprang up and competition to provide better, cheaper services across the country was fierce. In 1847 a more direct route from Stafford to London was provided by the Trent Valley Railway via Rugby, thus avoiding Birmingham. Presumably the London trippers to Palmer's execution would have been brought into Stafford along this line.

Of course, not everybody wanted the railways. Farmers were justifiably irate at the danger to their summer-ripe crops from engine sparks and they claimed too, that hens disturbed by the noise would refuse to lay. Horse breeders were concerned that their trade would disappear, and it certainly suffered a rapid decline with the demise of the stagecoach. Some simply thought it wrong to rush about at thirty miles an hour!

Although by the end of this century people had embraced the railways as the quickest and most comfortable method of conveyance, and the first motor cars were already on the roads, the most popular form of personal transport was the bicycle. In 1868 Daniel Rudge, a Wolverhampton innkeeper, set up a company to make velocipedes, otherwise known as the dandy-horse or the penny-farthing. During the next thirty years these extremely uncomfortable, difficult to handle, bone-shakers with a 5ft (1.5m) front wheel, progressed into something more instantly recognisable as a bicycle, with two equally sized wheels and pneumatic tyres. Rudge had died by then and his company was taken over by Whitworth Cycles who combined the two names, and from 1911 went on to manufacture motor cycles.

There is archaeological evidence to support coal mining in the County as long ago as the 2nd century AD and certainly they were digging coal in Sedgley in 1273 and on Cannock Chase in 1298. By the 14th century the West Bromwich and Wednesbury area were delivering coal to Oxfordshire and Northamptonshire, although it almost beggars belief that such a laborious task could have been viable given the primitive methods of transportation. By the end of the 17th century there was mining activity in most of the County but particularly where the seams outcropped or were shallow enough to be workable with the limited technology available at that time.

Then, with the new steam engines making it possible to keep the mines clear of water and to sink shafts deep enough to reach less accessible seams, new mining areas opened up in many parts of Staffordshire. The coal output, which in 1837 had been two million tons, was increased to eight million tons by 1870.

All this prodigious inventiveness during the first seventy years of the century did nothing to enhance the lot of the multitudes who still worked and lived in the mean, squalid, smoke polluted conditions that Boulton, Watt and Wilkinson had fostered in the previous century. In 1868 the American Consul in Birmingham, Elihu Burritt, wrote a book about the area and he called it 'The Black Country and its Green Borderland'. And so 'The Black Country' had arrived and the people that its harsh environment shaped had an identity that marked them out from others in their County. They developed their own culture, their own humour and their own dialects, and now - especially in the last thirty years, a fierce pride has developed in who they are and how their forebears fashioned the beginnings of today's modern world.

So that this heritage would never be lost, The Black Country Museum was established in the 1960s on land in Tipton so pitted with old, unmarked mine shafts that it was of no commercial use. There you can see a replica of Newcomen's steam pumping engine probably within a mile of the spot where the original one was built to serve Lord Ward's coal mine.

While the Black Country forged a place in history with its coal and heavy engineering, the County town made boots. The fertile pastures surrounding Stafford supported the cattle that supplied the leather upon which the industry developed. Shoemaking was recorded as a trade in the town in 1414 and by 1476 a Shoemaker's guild had been formed which regulated apprenticeships and imposed conditions on non-locals trading in the area. When Richard Brinsley Sheridan was MP for the Borough in 1780 he proposed a toast at an election dinner, "May the manufacturers of Stafford be trodden under foot by all the world." Sheridan is probably better remembered as a playwright than a politician; he wrote, among other works, 'The Rivals' and 'The School for Scandal'.

Staffordshire people were enormously proud of their 'homespun' Prime Minister, although, in fact, Robert Peel did not come to live at Drayton Bassett until he was ten years old in 1790. His father, a wealthy Lancashire cotton merchant, leased the Hall at Tamworth Castle as a forge and bought Drayton Bassett Manor where Robert grew up. The Castle, like so many others in Staffordshire, had been abandoned as a residence in the late seventeenth century.

Peel became a Tory M P when he was just twenty one years old, in 1829. He was Prime Minister twice and carried through wide ranging reforms to the criminal law and the prison system as well as founding the Metropolitan Police Force whose 'Bobbies' and 'Peelers' owe their nicknames to his memory.

Staffordshire clay figurines of Sir Robert Peel looming large on an out of scale horse were produced in their thousands in North Staffordshire and would have been on display in humble abodes across the County. They became somewhat prophetic because his death at sixty-two was as the result of a riding accident. He died at his home in Drayton Bassett and is buried in the churchyard there.

I have read that Tamworth pigs are golden haired and pink skinned; I have read that they are sandy red; and having examined them myself at Shugborough's Park Farm, as far as I am concerned, they are ginger. Fine, sturdy, ginger porkers! These striking

creatures were bred early this century reputedly from a wild Indian sow and a Hampshire boar. More than that I hesitate to tell you because the information seems so conflicting. I have been given three names each purported to be the original breeder, including Sir Robert Peel, who, I would have thought, was busy enough running the country without worrying about the nation's breakfast.

Whenever Sylvia and I discussed the embroideries she referred to this century as her 'transportation panel', an apt description when you look at the number of designs representing some form of mechanical conveyance.

Landlocked and with our unnavigable rivers, we may never have had any use for an 'Aaron Manby', but we certainly made full use of the canals once James Brindley and later, Thomas Telford pointed us in the right direction. Then the railways steamed promisingly into the 1830s and gave folk their first chance to see a world further away than the next village or town. The trusty steed suffered serious competition once the penny-farthing's front wheel shrunk to a manageable size, and then, the final blow to its long reign came in the final decade of the century with the motor car.

Just in time to be a part of the 19th century, Edward Lisle's Star car was first offered for sale in 1899 at a price of £198 which put it well beyond the reach of the working classes. Lisle had started off making velocipedes in the late 1860s and progressed through safety bicycles to motorcycles and then to the automobile all made from his Wolverhampton premises. The company prospered, boasting that they could produce a motor car from start to finish in just one week. In 1902 they produced their first van and then went on to manufacture a range of commercial vehicles. After the first World War they built a new factory in Showell Road, Bushbury, but within a decade, financial problems forced them to allow Guy Motors to take a controlling interest in the company which then struggled on until March 1932 when the Official Receiver was called in.

The ceremonial elephant, bejewelled and bedecked, signifies Great Britain's power in India. The defeat of Napoleon at Waterloo in 1815 left Britain the greatest power in Europe and supreme in the colonial world, where, even though we had lost our American colonies during the eighteenth century, we still owned the Canadian provinces, most of the West Indies, Africa and Australasia.

The Royal Titles Bill, passed by Parliament in 1876, made Victoria Empress of India. Disraeli was instructed by the Queen to make this happen because she believed that the title Empress of India would mean more to the Indian people than Queen of England - which was probably true. But there was another reason too; Victoria's eldest daughter Vicky had married the son of the Emperor of Germany which meant that when the Emperor died, she would become an Empress. Victoria couldn't have that!

The Closing Motif

The Nineteenth Century Embroidery Details

I could not work the Marquis of Anglesey in gold leather - he would have looked like King Midas; so I used stump work, a form of raised embroidery. This was a new technique to me, and I was pleased with the result.

I was constrained by the holes in the 12 count canvas when I came to working the spokes of the penny-farthing. The holes did not always allow the spokes to be completely symmetrical, although, I must say, no one has yet complained.

There was a lot of fiddly work involved in depicting the metalwork of the Galton Bridge - creating the three dimensional foliage at the front of the cameo took a myriad of different coloured threads.

The Twentieth Century Embroidery Details

The Beaudesert badge is the only motif not designed and crafted by myself. I was for many years a Guide leader and so I knew just how important badges can be!

The curlicues of the Armitage-Shanks loo bowl were far too intricate to work on even the finest of canvas, so I used linen. This was worked freehand from a design that the company sent me of an early twentieth century lavatory. The mahogany seat was embroidered in single thread satin stitch worked in an arc inthe shape of a loo seat.

Sir Stanley Matthew's face was worked on linen too, using satin stitch curved to the shape of the features in varying shades of flesh tone. The old-fashioned football was created in the same way as the lion of the twelfth century, padded and couched with gold braid.

The Twentieth Century

Kings and Queens of the Century

Edward VII (the Peacemaker) reigned 1901-1910. Married Princess Alexandra of Denmark, daughter of the King of Denmark.

George V (the Sailor King) reigned 1910-1936. Married Princess Mary of Teck.

Edward VIII (the Uncrowned King) reigned 325 days. As Prince of Wales, Edward was a frequent visitor to Himley Hall where the owners of Dudley Castle had long since transplanted themselves. His much publicised affair with the twice divorced American, Mrs Wallace Simpson, shocked a nation who had become used to the regal decorum of King George V's reign. Edward abdicated to marry his mistress.

George VI reigned 1936-1952. Edward VIII's brother. Married Lady Elizabeth Bowes-Lyon. George was the third monarch during 1936. His father, George V died on 20th January and his brother, Edward VIII abdicated less than eleven months later on 10th December.

Elizabeth II acceded to the throne when her father died in 1952. The Queen has already reigned for longer than her namesake Elizabeth I although she still has some way to go before she beats her great-great-grandmother's reign of 63 years 216 days.

The Borders

The Staffordshire Bull Terrier, although only recognised as a pedigree dog in 1935, has been around for over two hundred years. It was originally bred for blood sports such as bull baiting and dog fighting, and although these dreadful 'sports' were outlawed in 1835, the Staffordshire Bull Terrier is in no danger of losing its popularity, especially in the Black Country.

Sydney Guy gained much of his experience with the Sunbeam Motor Company where he was works manager while Louis Coatalen was designing his race-winning Sunbeam cars. The company, Guy Motors Ltd, was launched in 1914 from a factory at Fallings Park, Wolverhampton, and the distinctive Guy 'Indian Head' mascot came into use about ten years later. It became one of the most famous symbols in the vehicle world.

Although Guy specialised in making lorries, charabancs, and double-decker trolley buses, they still made cars and in 1919 a completely unsuspecting public was presented with the 20 mph Guy V8 motor car. The vehicle had been kept a perfect secret throughout its trials.

Most people know that Princess Anne drives a Reliant Scimitar, made by Reliant Cars who used to have a factory along the A5 at Tamworth. You couldn't miss the factory because there was a tall narrow building (originally it had been a mill) on the site, with RELIANT painted down the length of it. But how many people know that the Princess Royal actually learned to drive in a Reliant Robin? In fact, a Reliant Robin van still trundles around Gatcombe Park today.

The original three-wheeled van was the brain-child of a brilliant engineer named Thomas Williams, and the prototype came out of Thomas's back garden workshop in Tamworth on 1st January 1935.

During World War Two, war work took the place of vehicle production, as it did with other companies mentioned on this panel, but afterwards the factory reverted to vehicle manufacture and produced the three-wheeled Reliant Regal saloon car. Three years later in 1956 the fibre glass bodied Regal Mk II was introduced to an unsure public and mistrusting motor insurance underwriters.

By the time the Reliant Robin superseded the Regal in the early sixties there was already a 'Reliant public' who would not dream of abandoning their economically priced, low maintenance, cheap to run three-wheelers. Even the insurance underwriters, (a strange body of individuals whose by-word has always been 'if you don't know, double the premium') had come to accept that the word 'Reliant' wasn't synonymous with hefty claims, and had drastically reduced their premiums.

During the 1980s and the first half of the 1990s Reliant's fortunes were fraught with financial difficulties, but all this seems to be behind them now and I'm sorry to have to report to any of you who can't stand these little 'plastic pigs' that a new three-wheeled model, the Robin Hatchback was recently launched from new state-of-the-art premises at Burntwood, and this should take the company well into the millennium.

O n 2nd November 1874 the Midland Counties Evening Express became the first daily newspaper in Wolverhampton. Six years later the paper faced competition from a new arrival, the Evening Star. In 1884 these two newspapers amalgamated when the younger bought out its older rival and on 1st July the Evening Express and Star was launched.

The newspaper now prints approximately 200,000 copies daily and with a circulation area of 600 square miles it covers almost the whole of southern Staffordshire and parts of the West Midlands.

M any of the owners of landed estates found it impossible to maintain their stately homes after the First World War, when staff wages became a hopeless burden. Several homes were drastically reduced by dismantling a wing or two, while others buildings were completely demolished. The 6th Marquis of Anglesey (the descendant of the Paget whose leg was shot off at Waterloo) sold his Staffordshire lands and moved out of the County. The beautiful Elizabethan manor built by his forebears in the sixteenth century was knocked down in 1935.

The grounds of the estate now provide a permanent home for the Scout and Guide Association where young people from the four corners of the globe can stay and learn to enjoy a variety of sports and activities from abseiling to camping. Their badge, created especially to celebrate sixty years of Scouting and Guiding, enjoys the distinction of being the ONLY cameo not worked by Sylvia herself in the whole of the eleven panels.

At Beaudesert there is a building dedicated to one of Staffordshire's County Commissioners, Dorothy Dean who held office from 1946 until her tragic death in a road accident in 1953. Dorothy left the County a legacy and part of that has been used, along with a lottery grant, to purchase grounds at Hixon near Stafford for the Staffordshire Guide Association's permanent headquarters. The County Secretary worked from her home until 1986 when small, inconvenient premises in Stone were rented. Since the lease ran out at Stone, a disused classroom in Lonsdale County Primary School has served as an office, but from 22nd February 2000, for the first time in its history, the Staffordshire Guide Association will have their own purpose-built accommodation.

We left the Talbots back in Tudor times, when George the 6th Earl of Shrewsbury was worrying over the task of keeping Mary Queen of Scots out of mischief. The family suffered mixed fortunes during the next century. In the Civil War their castle became a parliamentary garrison and was severely damaged. Later, Charles, the 12th Earl, was one of seven signatories on the letter inviting William of Orange to come over and rule England in 1688. In the early 18th century, this same Charles signed the document proclaiming George I King of England and afterwards served him as Secretary of State.

In 1814, the 15th Earl, another Charles, began to enlarge Alton Lodge which stood on the other side of the Churnet Valley from his ruined Castle. His nephew, the 16th Earl, continued the building work, adding more towers and turrets to the fairy-castle home and enhancing its magnificent gardens which tumbled down the valley to the River Churnet. By the time he died in 1852, the 16th Earl had spent £1,000,000 on his project. Just five years later the 17th Earl died without an heir so that Alton Towers, for all its splendour, became annexed to the properties of the 3rd Earl of Ingestre - he became the 18th Earl of Shrewsbury - who already owned a magnificent Jacobean house, Ingestre Hall.

Like so many ancestral homes, Alton Towers became a financial burden to its owners after the First World War and in 1924 the estate was sold. Unlike Beaudesert, Alton Towers escaped the ultimate fate of being demolished, but during the Second World War it was occupied by troops who left it almost derelict. The Hall then stood neglected and crumbling while its grounds became a famous pleasure park. Now, due presumably to the great popularity of the pleasure park, Alton Towers management have been able to finance a full scale restoration including the refurbishment of the old gothic banqueting hall. I am told that the building will be ready to open in the year 2000 as a completely new and different attraction from anything else at the park.

On 20th April 1949 advancing communist forces shelled the frigate HMS Amethyst killing the Captain, injuring several crew and causing severe damage to the ship. Amethyst remained trapped in the head waters of the Yangtze River until 30th July when, under cover of darkness and with the crew now reduced to half rations, the ship began its escape to the open sea, a journey of 140 miles under almost constant enemy attack. Although there was one direct hit, at the end of the ordeal the ship's replacement Captain, Lieutenant Commander J S Kerans, signalled his famous message to the Admiralty, "Have rejoined the Fleet south of Woosung. No damage or casualties. God save the King." Surely at bit of propaganda!

Petty Officer George Griffiths of Hednesford was amongst the crew on that gallant dash to freedom and Sylvia remembers the excitement when he arrived home and stood on the balcony of a local pub to wave his sailor cap to the crowds who had turned out to welcome him - Hednesford's version of a civic reception!

Although it has nothing to do with Staffordshire, Sylvia, who is a great cat lover, thought you'd like to know that the Amethyst's moggy is the only cat ever to receive the Dickin medal, the animal's Victoria Cross. Daily, this saucy feline picked her way along the shelled superstructure of the ship, flicking her tail at the Chinese and improving the morale of the Amethyst's crew. She did, of course, protect the ships meagre food supplies from rodents too.

I've moved Jesse Pennington and Billy Wright down to make a trio with Stanley Matthews. Stanley and Billy were both young men that my grandfather, Jesse, watched 'coming through', years after he'd hung up his own boots.

The Panels

Staffordshire's most illustrious son - that is how Sylvia describes Sir Stanley Matthews - and so she has placed his portrait against an old fashioned leather football and given him pride of place as the opening cameo of this final panel of the Staffordshire Millennium Embroideries.

The Openinɢ Motif

Stanley's father was known as the 'Fighting Barber from Hanley' and he insisted on all of his sons following a rigid fitness regime, which meant that regular training was no hardship to the fifteen year old youth (schoolboy international winger) when he joined the Stoke City ground staff in 1930 with dreams of becoming a team player.

In May 1947 Stanley transferred to Blackpool (for £11,500). In 1953 he played in a match against Bolton which has gone down in history as the 'Matthews Cup Final.' Stanley passed a last minute ball to the Blackpool left winger who shot it straight into goal, winning the match and earning Stanley the Cup Winners Medal which had, until then, eluded him.

Towards the end of his career Stanley came 'home' to Stoke City to finish his brilliant career back with his original team. In fact, Stanley holds the record for being the oldest player in a First Division match when he appeared on 6th February 1965 for Stoke City against Fulham aged 50 years. He was voted Footballer of the Year in 1948 and 1963, and was European Footballer of the Year in 1956.

Billy Wright was turned away by the manager of Wolverhampton Wanderers, Major Frank Buckley, who told him that he was too small to become a professional footballer. Fortunately for Wolves, the Major changed his mind, and Billy, aged fourteen, was signed up in 1938 via Cradeley Heath for whom he scored a hat-trick to win three bars of chocolate. His debut in the Wolves first team was in November 1939 when he was still fifteen.

Two years later it looked as though he might never play football again when he broke his ankle in a cup-tie against West Bromwich Albion. However, even without the help of today's sophisticated medical support, the break quickly healed and Billy was back in business. He appeared in more than 650 games for Wolves, 490 in the Football League, and he became the first Englishman to win a century of international caps. Always popular, he became 'Footballer of the Year' in 1952 and seven years later, just a month before he retired, he was awarded the CBE for services to football.

Jesse Pennington was born in West Bromwich and played virtually all of his career for his home team. His first match for West Bromwich Albion was against Liverpool in 1903 and his last match, (his 445th league game), nineteen years later was against the same team. During his long career he captained 'The Baggies' from 1911 to 1922, and he twice captained England. He never lost his place in the Albion team, other than through injury, and his record of twenty seven Home Internationals held for fifty years until it was broken by another of our Staffordshire Millennium Football Stars, Billy Wright.

Jesse was my grandfather, and as there are so many family legends about him, I asked my nephew, his great-grandson to tell you his favourite:

When he was a small boy my great-grandfather helped a blind man sell newspapers around the Spon Lane area of West Bromwich and Smethwick by dribbling a tin can non-stop along the route. The story goes that once he set the can in motion he never lost control of it and the blind man walked behind following the clatter.

Chris Pennington, Essex.
August 1999

BOING BOING!
BAGGIES BAGGIES!

Giant Killers 1 - On Saturday 14th January 1933 Walsall who were in Division Three (N) battled their way into the third round of the F A Cup and there beat Arsenal 2 - 0. **Giant Killers 2 -** More recently, Hednesford Football Club (National Conference League) beat Blackpool (Division Two) 1 - 0 in the second round of the F A Cup. Then followed another 1 - 0 win against York City (Division Two) in the third round. On 25th January 1997 the team faced Premier Division Middlesborough in the fourth round at the Riverside Stadium, Middlesborough. Five minutes before the end of the game with a 1 - 0 score in Hednesford's favour, it looked almost certain that they were through to the fifth round, when two last-ditch-stand goals by Middlesborough scotched 'The Pitmens' dreams of Wembley.

This was the first time in the history of Hednesford FC that they had played against a Premier League club, but I have it on the best authority that the players don't intend it to be their last.

The world Queen Victoria left behind was changing fast. A popular scare story of the late 1800s - that by the beginning of the new century the roads would be impassable because they would be piled six feet high with horse dung - fizzled out with the advent of the motor car.

Once man had made the automobile reliable, he had to see how fast he could make it go, and it was just a few short years before cars were being built for the sole purpose of breaking speed records.

John Marston was a successful Wolverhampton bicycle manufacturer, but by 1901 his company had cautiously entered the automobile market with the Sunbeam Mabley. Four years later The Sunbeam Motor Company was formed to channel all efforts into making autocars.

During the First World War production switched to aero engines but afterwards Louis Coatalen, who had been the company's chief engineer since 1909, turned his talents back to cars, and particularly fast cars. He produced many racing vehicles, and on 29th March 1927, Major Henry Segrave set up a new record of 203.841 mph at Daytona Sands, Florida in a Wolverhampton made Sunbeam car.

Another Sunbeam racing car, the Silver Bullet, which was over thirty feet long and only three feet wide, was built with the intention of beating Segrave's previous record but the project was abandoned and the vehicle never actually raced on the Daytona Sands, nor did it ever claim any speed records.

Privately owned motor cars were going faster too by the 1920s and the need to have some control at crossroads was solved by the introduction of automatic traffic lights. The first set in the Country were installed in Wolverhampton at Princess Street, Five Ways, on 5th November 1927.

Just three days earlier, the Prince of Wales, (later Edward VIII, the Uncrowned King) having partied the night away with friends at Himley Hall, arrived, looking rather less than bright-eyed, and bushy tailed, to open the Birmingham New Road. Along the Coseley section of this tremendous engineering feat, a cherry tree was planted for each local man killed in the Great War. This sombre reminder of life's fragile nature did nothing to stop road hogs and speed merchants who kept the West Bromwich coroner busy with as many as ten inquests a year. After the traffic lights at Five Ways had proved their worth they were adopted all along this treacherous route in the 1930s.

While we are on the subject of speed still, I will mention the County's three Grand National winners. Over a period of twenty four years Tom Coulthwaite was successful three times with horses trained on Hednesford Hills:

1907: Eremon, a bay gelding won by six lengths. A remarkable feature of Eremon's success was that the jockey, A. Newey, lost an iron a mile from home and finished the race with one stirrup.

1910: Jenkinstown, another bay gelding and a long price winner at 100 to 8 managed to pull away and beat Jerry M, the favourite, by three lengths after they jumped the last fence together.

1931: Grakle, another bay gelding and another long price winner at 100 to 6. It was Grakle's fifth attempt at the Grand National and he did it by one and a half lengths.

There were many brave men connected with Staffordshire who were awarded Victoria Crosses during this century - as well as in the 19th century from the medal's instatement in 1854 - and Sylvia made a random choice of three of them.

John Henry Carless was born on 17th May 1896 in Walsall. He joined the Royal Navy as an Ordinary Seaman and was wounded in the abdomen whilst serving on HMS Caledon during the Battle of Heligoland on the 17th November 1917. Despite his injuries, twenty one year old Carless remained at his gun, helping and encouraging other casualties until he collapsed and died.

Lance-Corporal John Patrick Kenneally of the Irish Guards, was born in Birmingham on 15th March 1921. He married a Tipton girl and came to live and work in the Black Country. On 28th April 1943 whilst fighting in the Tunisian desert, Kenneally charged down a slope into the main body of the enemy who were about to attack, firing his Bren gun from the hip. On the 30th April, accompanied by a sergeant, Kenneally repeated his exploit and although wounded, he continued his assault and lived to receive his VC personally.

Lance-Sergeant John Daniel Baskeyfield of the South Staffordshire Regiment, 1st Airbourne Division, was born in Burslem on 18th November 1922. He was twenty one years old when he died on 20th September 1942 at Arnhem, Holland. In the course of an engagement where he was in charge of an anti-tank gun, Baskeyfield was injured and all of his crew were killed. He continued to man his gun until it was put out of action, then he crawled to another post and fired two shots, one of which was a direct hit, before he was killed.

On the night of Monday 31st January/1st February 1916, nine Zeppelins dropped 379 bombs on the Midlands. This was one of the heaviest raids of the War killing seventy people and injuring 113.

The enemy was in fact heading for Liverpool, but navigation of these early craft was difficult, and fog as they crossed the east coast of England, and again in the Trent Valley, probably caused confusion.

Burton suffered dreadfully that night with the Zeppelins flying overhead for more than an hour. The town was not considered a high risk target so there was no 'blackout' imposed and everywhere was well lit up, especially the cinema and the railway sidings. Fifteen people died of their injuries and another seventy two were seriously hurt.

Walsall's first attack that same evening started about forty five minutes earlier than the raid on Burton, and again there were no 'blackout' restrictions in operation, nor warning sirens. There was a second attack shortly after midnight. This ship, later identified as the L19 and commanded by Kapitanleutnant Loewe was the only Zeppelin not to return safely to Germany. L19, with a crew of seventeen, had joined in bombing Burton, and then Loewe directed his craft towards Birmingham, which was completely blacked out and so impossible for him to locate.

Instead, Loewe headed for Wednesbury, probably attracted there by fires started in a raid earlier in the evening. Just after midnight he flew over Ocker Hill Colliery, Tipton and dropped five bombs before attacking Dudley where most of his explosives landed in the castle grounds. The L19 then returned to Tipton where eleven high explosives landed roughly in the same area that had been devastated by another Zeppelin a few hours previously. The ship then returned for its second attack on the Walsall/Pleck area before heading for home. Captain Loewe and his crew never saw Germany again, the Zeppelin developed engine trouble and ditched into the North Sea.

R J Mitchell's 'low wing cantilever monoplane' may seem, at first glance a strange choice of subject for the centre piece of this, the final panel and when interviewed for a television programme about the embroideries, Sylvia explained her decision: "Well, Mitchell was a Staffordshire man; and we may not all be here today, enjoying the life style we do, if it hadn't been for his Spitfire."

Born in 1895, Reginald Joseph Mitchell showed a mean ability as a mathematician while still at Hanley High School and spurned his father's invitation to

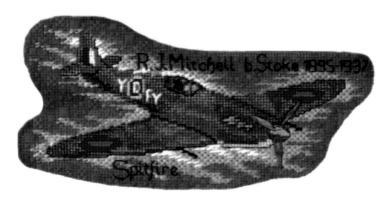

join the family printing business. After his apprenticeship with an engineering firm in Fenton, he joined Supermarine Aviation Works of Southampton and remained with them all his working life.

Over 20,000 Spitfires were built, and the one Sylvia depicts, with its squadron markings Y-FY, is one of 11,939 built at Castle Bromwich near Birmingham. This plane, built in 1940, went into operations at RAF Speke protecting the Liverpool docks and ended its service life at Turn Hill just over the border from Staffordshire.

Mitchell's 'thirty feet of wicked beauty' caught the war time public's imagination after young RAF pilots saved Britain from invasion in the summer and autumn of 1940. A national fund was set up so that people could help the war effort by 'presenting a Spitfire.' Amongst the many towns in the County who raised funds was Leek, where by January 1941 almost £5,800 had been collected. They called their Spitfire 'Spirit of Leek' and it was in service from May 1941 until February 1944. The Wolverhampton Express and Star launched a readers' fund which amassed £6,000 in just six days. A competition to name this Spitfire resulted in 'The Inspirer' being painted in 20 cm high yellow letters on the engine cowling.

Mitchell died in 1937 before the Battle of Britain so he never knew the vital role his Spitfire would play in saving the Nation. There seems to be some controversy over Reginald Mitchell's place of birth, so Sylvia contacted his son, Dr Gordon Mitchell, who states that his father was born in Stoke-on-Trent.

In the Commonwealth Cemetery at Broadhurst Green on Cannock Chase are the graves of seventy New Zealand soldiers who travelled half way across the world to assist the English fight a common cause. Sadly, many of these young men, having survived the war died in the Spanish Influenza epidemic of November 1918.

In 1959, a small valley of some 600 acres near to the Commonwealth Cemetery was transferred to the German War Graves Commission. German servicemen of two World Wars, whose remains were buried throughout England's churchyards, were brought to this communal resting place. This discreet operation during the early 1960s took over two years to complete and there are nearly 5000 graves there, each with a headstone of Belgian granite, tended by British gardeners. 20,000 German visitors come to this tranquil corner every year.

I have saved writing this piece until today, 4th August 1999, for a special reason. In 1953 when Her Majesty Queen Elizabeth the Queen Mother opened the Blithfield Reservoir during the South Staffordshire Waterworks Company's centenary year, it is unlikely that she ever considered the possibility of celebrating her own centenary. Today, the Queen Mum celebrates her 99th birthday and is looking chipper enough to see in the Millennium, and then go on another eight months to become the first English queen to become 100 years old.

The South Staffordshire Water Company came into being in 1853 to provide a pure and plentiful water supply to the industrialised Black Country. This century's increased awareness of hygiene and sanitation caused the demand to increase dramatically and the water authority were granted permission to construct a reservoir on the River Blithe at Blithfield near Rugely in 1939. World War Two delayed the undertaking and work was not begun until 1947. The reservoir holds 18,170 million litres of water and covers an area of 790 acres. Although a sizeable chunk of Bagot Park was submerged, the view from the Bagots' home, Blithfield Hall was certainly enhanced by magnificent lake views through the parkland trees.

This, the largest body of water in Staffordshire, has become an established nature reserve and the South Staffs Waterworks have joined forces with English Nature and the Staffordshire Wildlife Trust in a regeneration programme which has involved planting thousands of trees, hazel, holly, silver-birch, mountain ash, and of course, Staffordshire's indigenous oak.

While I am on the subject of supplying water for the County's increasing requirements, it seems an appropriate time to mention the biggest name in the smallest room in the house - Armitage Shanks, manufacturers of sanitary ware since 1851.

A Public Health Act passed in 1848 dictated that all new houses must have a 'sufficient water closet or privy or ashpit' and so, suddenly there was a legal requirement for sanitary ware. At about the same time as the Act, Salt and Swan acquired a bankrupt pottery factory in the village of Armitage near to the Trent and Mersey canal and started to supply lavatories in response to the new law's demand.

When Sylvia was speaking to the Heritage Manager about sponsorship of the twentieth century panel, he happened to mention that the Company had not always been Armitage Shanks. "From 1867 until 1960 we were Edward Johns," he told her. "Ah," said Sylvia, "is that why......?"

So there you are folks, now you know why the Loo is called the John. This, of course begs the question as to why the John is called the Loo!

Sylvia's intricately embroidered lavatory would have been in a rather posh house around the turn of the century and would probably have been ordered with a wash basin to match. By the 1920s the elaborate decoration and mouldings - which weren't really a good idea because they harboured bacteria and dirt, had been replaced by plain, functional white glazed WCs.

In 1960 the name of the company was changed from Edward Johns Ltd to Armitage Ware Ltd and then, at the end of the decade they merged with Shanks Holding Ltd to form the Armitage Shanks Group Limited. The Company, with its head office still in the picturesque village of Armitage, where oak beamed pubs are more the norm than commercial institution headquarters, trades from eight different UK sites, mostly in Staffordshire and supplies the world with heavy duty industrial sanitary ware as well as domestic bathroom and kitchen appliances under the name of Armitage Shanks.

For 62 year old ship's captain, Commander Edward John Smith, the maiden voyage of the Titanic was to be his last trip before retirement. During his long career, Smith had sailed over two million miles and he was the highest paid captain in the world, on an annual salary of £1250.

The Titanic, a 'floating luxury hotel', was said to be unsinkable because of the novel design of its hull. It had a top speed of 23 knots and on this first Atlantic crossing it was carrying 2227 passengers and crew.

The ship left Southampton on 10th April 1912. During Sunday 14th April ice warnings were received from other ships in the area, and that evening Captain Smith and the Second Officer discussed the fact that the calm weather made the detection of icebergs difficult because the lack of wind or tell-tale surf.

The Captain retired to his cabin at 9.20pm. Just before 11.40pm, lookouts in the crow's nest noticed a slight haze, but they were unable to make it out - the ship's-binoculars had been left behind in Southampton. Minutes later the ship hit an iceberg. By midnight Captain Smith had assessed the damage and he knew that the Titanic was sinking. He ordered the lifeboats to be loaded - 'women and children first'. People were reluctant to leave the ship and Lifeboat 28 was lowered holding only 24 women and four crew. The women begged Captain Smith to allow some of the husbands into the lifeboats to row, but 'women and children only' was the order. As all the lifeboats rowed away from the stricken ship there were still 1522 people left on board, and John Smith made his way back to the bridge to await his fate as Captain of the ship.

The Captain's bronze statue has been surrounded by controversy ever since his 12 year old daughter unveiled it on 29th July 1914. Smith was from the Potteries - born in Hanley - so why, people ask, is his statue in Lichfield. There are two stories:

Early in 1913 it was proposed that a memorial to Captain Smith be placed in Lichfield. A petition objecting to this, mainly on the grounds that the Commander had no real connection with the City, was rejected, and his statue was erected in Beacon Park. The Lichfield Mercury explained to its readers that Lichfield was the diocese of Smith's birth, and also that the City was a convenient calling place for visitors from London and Liverpool.

Secondly, Staffordshire folklore persists with the story that Hanley rejected the statue because much of the blame for the disaster had been layed at the Captain's feet. His daughter said 50 years later, 'I seem to remember something about a town rejecting the statue'. Make what you will of it! It seems odd, though, that the statue's inscription made no mention of the Titanic - until May 1985 when the words 'Captain Smith was Captain of the Titanic' were added.

Mines rescue teams were called upon to deal with many dramas and disasters in the coalfields of the North and South Staffordshire but none as strange as that asked of the Hednesford Mines Rescue Team just before the Second World War.

One hundred and three men were aboard the submarine, the Thetis, at 10.00am on 1st June 1939 when she set out from Birkenhead on her sea trials. Extra to the normal crew were eight naval officers who commanded their own submarines - they had joined the new vessel to witness its performance. There were also extra electricians, ship and engine fitters, two employees of a catering firm and the Mersey Pilot, swelling the ship's crew.

At 3.00pm and 38 miles from land, the Thetis sank. Four men were able to escape; two others drowned attempting to do so; the remaining ninety seven died from lack of oxygen inside the submarine.

When the vessel was eventually beached the navy were faced with another problem. They did not have the knowledge or the equipment to recover the bodies that had been trapped inside for 164 days. The Hednesford Mines Rescue team, with their specialist equipment and experience in coping with mine disasters were called in to deal with this sad and gruesome task.

There were many dramatic and sad mining disasters in both the North Staffordshire and South Staffordshire coalfields, with many hundreds of miners losing their lives, especially in the later years of the 19th and the first quarter of the 20th centuries. There were still 22 working collieries in the Potteries area alone in the mid 1950s, but the national policy of contraction in the industry saw the last coal mine in Staffordshire close at Silverdale at the end of 1998.

Mines Rescue teams were maintained at many of the collieries. Many stories of heroism were associated with them and the teams were often forced to make the harshest of decisions. On the morning of 1st April 1957 a new piece of equipment was being used at the Jubilee Colliery in West Bromwich. The machine, known as 'The Slasher', was designed to make the extraction at the coal face easier, but the extra vibration it caused led to a roof fall trapping thirty-five year old Jack Horler. The Mines Rescue Team were called in and set about trying to reach Jack who was still alive. The trapped man's brother, Joe, begged to go down with the team but they refused to take him. They knew a second fall was likely and if it became necessary to leave the area he would refuse to leave his brother and go with them. Sadly the second fall did occur and Jack was killed.

Shortly before 11.10am on November 27th 1944 there was an explosion at Fauld near Hanbury that was recorded by seismographic equipment as far away as

Casablanca. 4000 tons of bombs stored by the Air Ministry in the disused gypsum mines exploded causing the biggest blast in the world before the atom bomb was dropped on Hiroshima.

An estimated 68 people were killed although it was not possible to establish the exact death toll as at least eighteen people thought to have been in the area were never found. A 300 acre farm, Upper Castle Hayes, completely disappeared into the 150 foot deep crater ripped out of the Earth's crust, leaving no trace of man, beast, machinery or even trees.

It was said at the time that had it not been that the explosives were stored so deep in the mine, the explosion would have wiped out everything between Burton-on-Trent and Uttoxeter.

AJ Wilkinson of Burslem bought out Newport Pottery in the mid 1920s and acquired, along with the factory, a huge amount of dated and defective ware. One of the Wilkinson employees, Clarice Cliffe, suggested that in order to make these artefacts saleable, they should be covered with bright colours and designs. The idea was an enormous success and Clarice Cliffe's hand-painted Bizarre ware became one of the most important Art Deco ceramic designs of the 1930s.

Born in the potteries in 1899, Clarice started work as an apprentice in the enamelling trade at thirteen. She learned how to paint pottery free-hand, the art form that lead to her later success. She was seventeen when she moved to Wilkinsons and after four years the directors realised the young woman's great potential and moved her to work alongside their top designers in the decorating shop. A decade later, Clarice was made Wilkinson's art director and supervised a staff of over a hundred young decorators who learned to paint her amazing designs.

It seems incredible now to think that four years ago hardly anyone was interested in Sylvia's embroideries. But, back in the summer of 1996 would-be sponsors did not believe that one person, working unaided, could complete the task that Sylvia assured them was within her capabilities.

On the brink of despair she contacted JCB who, almost to her disbelief, said that they might be interested. "Could you depict one of our famous yellow machines?" they asked. Sylvia, rather taken aback, said that she would 'have a go' if they sent her an illustration. The postman handed her a bulky package a couple of days later - it was a JCB digger engineering specification! From this, Sylvia designed her graphic and, fingers crossed, sent it off for approval. Within the week confirmation arrived that, provided the digger held a prominent place on the 20th century panel, they would sponsor her work.

That, folks, is why a huge, solid, uncompromising, yellow digger graces - did I say graces? - this panel; Sylvia's grateful acknowledgement to the fact that if it had not been for JCB the Staffordshire Millennium Embroideries might never have come to fruition. Having said that, what more appropriate way to bring a history of Staffordshire to a close. Staffordshire has been a county of great industrial inovation, individuality and success for several hundred years. JCB is a highly successful British company, employing 3,500 people at its Staffordshire factories in Rocester, Uttoxeter and Cheadle, and worldwide.

30th September 1999. The embroideries are finished. Sylvia has laid down her needle and scissors - I hope; and I can think of no better way to end this book than with Sylvia's final closing motif and her own poem: